T0286842

Praise for
Relationship Road Map

"*Relationship Road Map* is more than just words printed on a page—it's a glimpse into the way I know Stephen Chandler leads his life: with faith, tenacity, and practicality. This book is a helpful resource for anyone looking to find the right one or looking to align their relationship with God's heart."

—TIM TIMBERLAKE,
senior pastor of Celebration Church

"Perhaps one of Stephen Chandler's greatest gifts is taking complex ideas and making them into simple yet comprehensive steps you can walk out in your everyday life. *Relationship Road Map* is a masterful example of that skill. This book has taken an immense task and turned into a road map that anyone can follow. I'm excited to see the impact this book will have on its readers."

—DR. DHARIUS DANIELS,
lead pastor of Change Church
and host of *The Dharius Daniels Podcast*

Relationship Road Map

Relationship Road Map

Step-by-Step Directions to Finding Your Spouse

Stephen Chandler

Details in some anecdotes and stories have been changed to protect the identities of the persons involved.

Library of Congress Cataloging-in-Publication Data
Names: Chandler, Stephen, author.
Title: Relationship road map: turn by turn directions to finding your spouse / Stephen Chandler.
Description: First edition. | [Colorado Springs, CO] : WaterBrook, [2025] | Includes bibliographical references.
Identifiers: LCCN 2024034808 | ISBN 9780593194287 (hardcover) | ISBN 9780593194294 (ebook)
Subjects: LCSH: Single people—Religious life. | Dating (Social customs)—Religious aspects—Christianity. | Marriage—Religious aspects—Christianity.
Classification: LCC BV4596.S5 C43 2025 | DDC 248.8/4—dc23/eng/20240927
LC record available at https://lccn.loc.gov/2024034808

Printed in the United States of America on acid-free paper

waterbrookmultnomah.com

2 4 6 8 9 7 5 3 1

First Edition

Book design by Susan Turner

For details on special quantity discounts for bulk purchases, contact specialmarketscms@penguinrandomhouse.com.

To my amazing wife, Zai. While we may disagree on whether our first date was at the crusty diner with week-old pie or the carriage ride through Philadelphia, ending at the Cuban restaurant, one thing is for sure: This journey with you has been the greatest joy of my life. Thank you for teaching me a love I never knew was humanly possible. I will love you forever and like you for always!

Contents

Introduction

Are You Ready for This Journey?

NOWADAYS, THE ONLY WAYS YOU CAN GET LOST WHILE DRIVING are if you leave your phone at home, if it dies and you don't have a way to charge it, or if you find yourself visiting one of the rare places on the globe without cell service. Otherwise, it's impossible.

And yet some of us still get lost.

That's not how it was back in the day. Before we had GPS on our phones, there was MapQuest. If you entered your current location and your destination into this desktop computer site, you were able to print written directions to guide you. And before MapQuest, there were *paper maps*. Your parents or grandparents may have traveled with a huge map that got folded down to the size of a small book. So having a co-pilot was vital—if you didn't have someone to read the directions while you were driving, you would miss an exit. And God help you if you missed a turn, because there was no GPS with that British voice that promises, "Recalculating." Paper doesn't recalculate.

Dating for the purpose of finding that person you will marry is a journey.

A lot of us have never typed in our current location. On the dating journey, you identify your current location when you take stock of where you are, *right now,* and how you got here.

These are my hopes.

These are my dreams.

This is how my heart was broken in my last relationship.

These are the ways I may have a tainted view of dating and marriage based on my aunt's divorce. Or my parents' marriage.

Most of us haven't paused to really take stock of where we are today.

And perhaps you've never identified your desired *destination.* You may know vaguely that you want to be married or married again, but you might not be clear on exactly what you want that marriage to look like. What that destination will be.

There are important questions to consider for that future destination:

How will we help each other achieve our hopes and
   dreams?

How loving and affectionate will our marriage be?

Will we be one of those couples who after twenty years
   still can't keep our hands off each other?

How often will we have sex? (Hopefully that's not too
   direct for you. It may not be the first thing you think
   about—even though it probably is if you're a guy.)

Will we stay up late into the night and have wonderful
   conversations dreaming about what the future may
   hold?

How will we manage our money?

What will be our standard of living?

Who will do the majority of the cooking? Are we going fifty-fifty?

How often are we going to vacation?

If we do have kids, will we both work or will one of us stay home with them?

So many unknowns! And if we're on a first date or a fifth date with someone, we may not know how to discern where we are in the journey.

We don't know if we've taken a wrong turn.

We don't know when we should abandon the journey and go back home.

We don't know when we've arrived at the destination.

There's vital information we need before embarking on this journey called dating-toward-marriage.

The Only Reason You Should Be on the Road

Before we launch, I want to make one thing clear: The only reason to date is to find the partner, the co-pilot, you will spend the rest of your life with. And I know that's a rare opinion. This may be the first time you are hearing this, but don't shut me out.

If you're a woman, your girls are probably telling you to date so you can get a free meal and not be at home with your cat every weekend.

If you're a man, your boys may be telling you that you should date to get a lil' somethin' somethin'. Hopefully your Christian friends are not saying this. (But let's be real, some of them are.)

However, I want to you to have real clarity and conviction as you start this journey. The only reason to be dating at all is to find the person you will marry. I believe God's design for romantic relationships between men and women is for them to move toward marriage. And God designed marriage to be a picture of Christ's relationship with the church.[1] In other words, God designed dating to lead to a Christlike marriage, and a Christlike marriage is one of the primary ways God demonstrates the glory of the gospel to the world. So, our culture's view of dating—dating with little-to-no intention of pursuing marriage, dating just for fun, or dating for years without considering marriage—is directly contrary to God's design.

I know that may sound foreign and antiquated, but let me explain. First, you're fooling yourself if you think you can give someone your time but not give them your heart or get emotionally attached. Matthew 6:21 says, "Where your treasure is, there your heart will be also." Your greatest treasure is your time. Even if it's just your time, dating someone will always cost you. The person you date will have a piece of your heart. The inevitable disappointment from every breakup will ever so slightly callous your heart. I also believe that God designed sex to be enjoyed in the context of marriage, and it's already extremely difficult for many of us to maintain integrity and not sleep with the person we are dating. Removing the finish line of marriage and the reward of waiting increases our likelihood of falling.

Second, dating is time-consuming and requires investment. When you're investing your resources in one place, it means you're not investing elsewhere. I've seen so many people waste years of their lives—neglecting their personal growth or career advancement or their pursuit of their God-given purpose—all for someone they knew they wouldn't spend the rest of their life with. So, if marriage is not your objective, you really don't need to be wasting your time or theirs dating. I know you may be ticked off at me right now. I can live with that. Just keep reading.

To the Men on the Journey

If you're a man, I want us to be on the same page.

One of my biggest frustrations is a man who has finished college, or has already started his career, who tells me, "Pastor, I'll probably get married one day, but I'm not looking for a wife right now. I'm just chilling."

What is wrong with you?

Seriously, if you're an adult man and you desire to be married but aren't pursuing it, either you are living in sin—and that's why you're chilling, because you've got all your needs met—or your priorities are grossly out of whack.

And this guy might offer an explanation, such as, "You understand, man. I'm just trying to get my career off the ground."

Have you not read the Bible? The Bible says there is one thing that is really hard to find, and that's a virtuous and capable wife. I love the way *The Message* translation says it: "A good woman is hard to find, and worth far more than diamonds."[2] Not "A good job is hard to find." You can find that in any city in this country. But someone you can build the rest of your life with? That's rare and hard to find.

So many men have a tainted view of marriage. They've given in to the idea that a wife is an unnecessary hassle. These men hear the phrase that married folks love to throw around— "Happy wife, happy life"—and think that their next forty-plus years will be consumed with trying to make someone happy who is impossible to please. The Bible never says a wife is hard to find. It says a good wife. A virtuous wife. A woman with noble character. If you find a "good" wife, you've found a woman who will launch you into a level of influence, joy, and fulfillment that you would never be able to achieve without her. That type of woman is *hard* to find but is one thousand percent worth the search. Start looking now. If you're an adult and God has not called you to celibate singleness, you need to be ready to date with intention.

Another cause for hesitation may be a fear of commitment. Maybe you have built the habit of sleeping with people you are dating and know that you currently are not capable of being committed to one person in marriage. Maybe you've been married before or experienced a tough breakup and trusting someone again isn't something you can comprehend right now. Whatever your situation, I would encourage you not to sit in your fears. Let's do the work to get to the place where you are not only ready for the commitment but also excited for it. Hopefully I can stir up some holy jealousy in you. You have no idea what a good and beautiful thing it is when you find the right person to do life with.

To the Women on the Journey

If you're a woman, I want to encourage you as you embark on this journey.

If you feel like you are a good catch, what do you do when there is absolutely *no one* in sight and it seems like no one is noticing you? Do you just sit and wait? Absolutely not.

I'm going to suggest that you do what Moses did in the desert. Before God ever called him to lead the Israelites out of

Egypt, Moses was in a season of development. Preparation. Today you are in a season of preparation. God intends to prepare you spiritually, to make you complete in Him. Ideally, you're also preparing financially by getting out of debt. You're taking care of your physical well-being; you're caring for your body and not allowing intimate access to men who have not committed to honoring you "'til death do us part."

Sister, I believe God gives us the desires of our hearts. But there are seasons of waiting. Of testing. And your attitude matters during this time. So, while you're waiting, serve. Get busy serving the church, your family, and your friends.

You may say, "I am doing all that. Now what?" I know that it can seem pretty rough on these streets. Maybe you've been putting yourself out there, but all the men you have dated thus far haven't been husband material. Maybe you're not seeing any options, and it's been a while since you've gone on a date. Maybe you live in a small town or attend a small church, and you feel like you've exhausted the options in terms of godly men in your area. Maybe you were dating someone who seemed like the perfect guy, only to be deeply let down by him or even utterly betrayed. Maybe you're recently divorced, widowed, or just past the age that you think is ideal for marriage. I don't care what statistics say. I don't care what our culture says. I know God's Word says that "no good thing will he withhold from them that walk uprightly."[3] Hold on to those words more tightly than you hold on to whatever statistics you see in the news or on TV or in a book, or whatever foolishness you hear from your bitter auntie. As believers, we live by faith and not by sight.

"Uh, but, Pastor, I don't see any prospects."

That's right where you need to be. You're living by faith and not by sight.

Later in this book, we will talk about how to position yourself and identify a potential lifelong partner. Don't neglect building a great life for yourself and pursuing your God-given purpose and potential. Marriage is amazing, but you don't need a partner to start living. Maximize this season of your life to the glory of God.

I want to encourage you to hold out for the man God has for you. When you're *ready* to be married, I know it can be tempting to consider settling. You may think about settling for the guy who's successful, charismatic, and interested in you but who is not walking with God and can't lead you and the family you hope to have one day. Don't compromise out of fear of being alone. God is faithful.

If you are grown and God has not called you to celibate singleness, you also need to be ready to date with intention.

To All the Singles on the Road

If you're single and would like to be married, this is a time of preparation. So, before you meet the person who will be yours, this is the season to be living well. You're becoming the person God made you to be. And as you wait in faith, you can have the confidence that—while you'd like to be married—you don't need marriage to *define* you. (But I don't mean that in a "I don't need a man" or "I don't need a woman" kind of way.) When you are secure in God, when your identity is anchored in Him, then you're ready to embrace this journey toward marriage. And you're ready to be *all in*.

Where We're Headed

If you're single and desire to be married, I want to journey with you. I believe God wants a good, healthy, beautiful, life-giving, challenging-yet-rewarding, Christlike marriage for you. I really do. Getting there, however, is going to require some intentionality. You need a plan. I would like to walk you through the various mile markers—talking, dating, engagement, marriage—to help you journey well. Specifically, I want you to pay attention to your pace, and I want you to notice the signs along the way. For example, if you're just getting to know someone, stay in the slow lane. You don't need to be hanging out together *every* night. Have fun. Take it slow. You may feel like this person is solid, and you may move to the middle lane. Your relationship might pick up a bit of momentum as you're dating. And if you're in that fast lane, heading toward marriage? That's when you really need to be paying attention to *all the signs*. (And if you're three years into dating someone and still in the slow lane? Start looking for an exit.)

My friend, I care about you. And I want God's best for you. If it's hard to see the road ahead, I got you. My hope is that this book can be a road map to get you to the destination of your dreams.

I'm confident that God has good in store for you.

—*Pastor Stephen*

Relationship Road Map

Begin with Your Destination in Mind

Know Where You Want to End Up

ABOUT FOUR YEARS AGO, I GOT SOME GREAT NEWS THAT HAD THE potential to impact my life in an extremely good way. When I found out, I knew I needed to stay dignified about it. Stay humble. I wasn't about to go on Instagram and holler, "I'm on top of the world!"

You know what I did in my house when I got that news? I turned on "So Fresh, So Clean" by Outkast, jumped up onto the kitchen countertop, and started shaking what my mama gave me. Guess what my wife, Zai, did? She jumped onto that countertop with me, and we screamed and danced and cut up and had the time of our lives. I want that for you! I want you to have someone to twerk on the kitchen countertop with for the rest of your life. This process of finding the right person to spend your life with is one of the greatest and most important endeavors you can embark on next to knowing Christ. Why? Because . . .

Life. Is. Amazing.

Life. Is. Hard.

Life is full of so many wonderful ups, but it's also filled with some really difficult downs. When you have someone on your best days to share the joy, it makes a great day one thousand times better. But sometimes you'll be curled up on the couch together in front of the fire, crying your eyes out after a difficult day. Having an amazing person who is committed to you for life on those days is one of the greatest joys a person could have. Remember that the first thing God declared *not* good was for "man to be alone."[1] This tells us that marriage is good. And while not everyone is called to get married, marriage is one of God's most profound gifts to us. Dating, with the goal of finding God's person for you, can be tricky, but I'm here to tell you that the journey you're on is *worth it*. There are few greater joys on planet earth—outside of your relationship with God—than finding your person and building an amazing marriage.

When you've got a lover you can cut up with, it makes all the difference. The way Zai and I cut up is absolutely ridiculous sometimes. The Bible says that laughter is like medicine, and in a healthy marriage, you have someone to laugh with.[2] You'll have your inside jokes, your secret handshakes. You were made to enjoy life with that person as long as you both live. The first relationship God established, after a relationship with Himself, was between a husband and a wife. And God created that union to be *good*.

This doesn't mean that there won't be difficult days. But it does mean that the number of those days will be cut in half.

Had a hard day at work? In conflict with a friend? Get a scary diagnosis? There is someone at home who will hold you, encourage you, and feed you apple pie after one of those bad days. That person is in your corner. They'll listen to you. And this person is also going to double your good days! Dancing on our kitchen countertop with Zai? My joy was doubled. When you've got a committed lover in your corner, your bad days are cut in half and the good ones are *more* than doubled.

You've also got someone to build with. God hasn't given every gift to every person. In fact, I think that God purposefully doesn't give you all the tools you need to fulfill your destiny. He has placed some of the tools you lack in your spouse! For example, I'm proud to be an introvert; I think we have the deepest relationships with others. The number of people who introverts know can be limited because of our discomfort in engaging new people. In ministry, what I started to find was that Zai would bring people into our world with her beautiful extroversion. That expanded our sphere of influence in our community. It expanded our support system. You hear it? I benefited from a gift I didn't possess. My partner is gifted in ways I am not. She has experience I don't. And that has been a blessing in all that God has called us to build.

I mentioned that life is hard, right? It's full of setbacks, disappointments, delays. And sometimes you can get discouraged and overwhelmed. In marriage, you have someone who can cheer you on and pick you up and remind you of the days that you won. When you're married, you have someone gifted by God to inspire and encourage you to accomplish the plan God has for you. When my strength is faltering, Zai is there for me and vice versa.

Have you ever seen a video of two people driving a stake or post into the ground? They might be setting up a tent or driving the spike on a train track. You'll see that one person will hit the top with a sledgehammer and then the other person takes a turn. Then the first person again. And while one person is hitting it, the other person is winding up. And next thing you know, they've got this rhythm of hitting it over and over and over and over. That stake gets driven into the ground so quickly because there are two hammers heading in the same direction. I love what the Bible says in *The Message* translation of Ecclesiastes 4:9–10: "It's better to have a partner than go it alone. Share the work, share the wealth. And if one falls down, the other helps."

Finally, in marriage, you have an ally who can watch your back. Because the Enemy doesn't want to see you accomplish the plans God has for you. And when the Enemy attacks our house? I have a wife who is watching my back, and I am watching hers. We cover each other in prayer. Not only does she pray for me, but she is also vigilant, watching for people who may be sent by the Enemy to take advantage of me, drain my energy, or distract me from or undermine God's call on my life. Zai senses it, and she warns me. You better believe I am doing the same for her, though not in an overprotective or jealous-husband type of way; I'm prayerfully looking for the people divinely sent by God to advance my wife toward her calling and watching out for those who are not.

While there is no foolproof plan for finding the perfect spouse, I believe that if you will date with intentionality and purpose, God's got somebody who is going to blow your mind and give above and beyond all that you can ever ask, think, or imagine. So as you begin this journey of dating—or you decide to reset the way you've been dating after reading this book!—I want you to travel with the destination in mind. God made marriage to be *good*.

If you follow the road map, you will get there.

And when you get there, you need to arrive in good shape. That means I want you to check your engine *now,* as you begin the journey, so that your eventual partner is meeting someone who is—at least *relatively*—whole and healthy and thriving. Keep reading to discover how!

Lies You May Hear About Marriage and Parenting

It's fine for married couples to sleep in separate rooms or even live in separate houses.

Co-parenting is easier than committing to someone in marriage.

Your lustful habits will instantly be resolved once you're married.

Getting married will solve all your single-life problems (financial problems, emotional issues, co-dependent relatives, life planning, loneliness, travel aspirations, and everything in between).

Check Your Engine

Don't Start the Journey Deficient

AS A CHILD, SARAH ALWAYS CAME TO SCHOOL WITH A SMILE AND excelled academically, so her teachers never suspected what she faced inside the walls of her home. Sarah, now twenty-five years old, had grown up with a father who served in the military from the age of eighteen until he retired at fifty-five, a decade after she was out of the home. We are all shaped by our parents' presence *and* our parents' absence, and Sarah was no different. Because her father often spent long stretches of time away from the family, she didn't know what it was like to have a father who was reliably present in the home, day in and day out. And when he was home? Sarah's father brought a lot of rage and violence into her life—a result of his own difficult childhood and the impact of the atrocities he'd witnessed in the military. And while he didn't physically harm her, Sarah witnessed her mother being abused.

Not only were Sarah's teachers unaware of the challenges she faced, but most of the men she dated later—who saw the same beautiful smile her teachers had seen—didn't suspect the trauma she'd endured either.

We've All Got Some Mileage on Us

Before a single person enters a marriage, he or she has done some living.

Maybe, like Sarah, she never saw a healthy marriage.

Maybe he grew up in a broken home.

Maybe she endured the trauma of an abortion.

Maybe he grew up with a parent who abused substances.

Maybe her parents told her she was stupid.

What that means is that all of us who were raised by imperfect parents are trying to create something that we've never seen before. And we're dragging around the baggage we've been accumulating along the way.

Now, I'm not saying that disqualifies you from a strong, healthy marriage. But if neither you nor your partner have done any work to get healthy, you'll be standing at the altar as two broken people. And two broken people can't make a whole marriage. When you enter into marriage, you've got to be whole in yourself. You have to decide to say, "I'm going to let God rebuild me. I'm going to let God restore me. I'm going to let Him remake me. I'm going to let Him bring back what the Enemy stole." The message I hear throughout the Bible is that God can redeem anything you've been through. God can restore. God can heal. And God can make whole. He can create purpose where there was pain.

Drs. Les and Leslie Parrott, authors of *Healthy Me, Healthy Us,* exhort people who are married to do one thing: *Get healthy.* In fact, they have boiled down their relationship advice into one sentence: "If you try to build intimacy with another before you have gotten whole on your own, all your relationships become an attempt to complete yourself."[1] When you're not whole, you look for someone else to complete you, but God didn't create anyone with that capability.

At most weddings you've likely heard Genesis 2:24: "That is why a man leaves his father and mother and is united to his wife, and they become one flesh." But I need you to hear: It's not half of a broken person (bringing their insecurities, fears, regrets, and hang-ups) joining with another half of a broken person (bringing their pride, anger, and lust). If we believe that the marriage equation is about addition—two halves making a whole—we're fooling ourselves. It's actually multiplication. Two whole people join to make a whole marriage:

$$1 \times 1 = 1$$

But two people who are incomplete? Two people who are halves? When they join, they do not create a whole:

$$0.5 \times 0.5 = 0.25$$

Being whole does not mean you're perfect. All of us are works in progress. Wholeness simply means you have reached a level of emotional health where you're not looking for another person to complete you but are finding your identity in Christ. Your relationships can only be as healthy as you are.

The problem is that we're looking for somebody to complete us, to heal us, to give us purpose, to give us a reason, to give us motivation.

Ladies, if your identity is linked to another person's opinion, you will rely on your boyfriend to make you feel beautiful. If he's a great guy, he'll try to make you believe you are. The problem is that no matter how many times he tells you you're beautiful, it will be hard for you to believe him. And that's if he's a great guy. If he's not a great guy, he will use your brokenness to get you to compromise your standards and integrity.

Gentlemen, if you aren't on your way to wholeness, you will rely on her to make you feel like a man. This will either put an impossible burden on her or even cause you to act in a domineering and selfish way as you try to prove something to yourself and to a world that wasn't questioning you to begin with.

I understand that many people are fearful of marriage, relationships, and commitment because they've witnessed others who have followed conventional approaches and experienced failure. And so, you might naturally think, *If Mom and Dad couldn't do it . . .* or *If that pastor couldn't do it . . .* or *If that person I admire couldn't do it . . . then who am I to think that it could work for me?*

Listen: It will work if you and your potential spouse do it God's way. I promise. Deuteronomy 31:6 exhorts, "Do not be afraid or terrified because of them, for the LORD your God goes with you; he will never leave you nor forsake you."

Don't Enter Deficient

My friends know I like driving my car with the gas tank as close to empty as possible. Well, it's not that I "like" it, but I really hate the inconvenience of slowing down to fill up. I won't lie: Driving on "E" can be stressful. I'm always wondering how many miles I have left before my car ends up disabled on the side of the road. And while I've not yet been stranded, the anxiety really takes away from the joy of the journey.

As you start this journey, I'm asking you to check your engine and fill your tank. Pay attention to those dashboard lights. Specifically, if you launch into dating without addressing your emotional health, it's going to be a miserable journey—for you *and* others. And you know where the state of your current emotional health began? It began in the family you grew up in.

God's good intention is for us to experience a sense of belonging and completeness within our families. This is part of our design. We are meant to receive love, affirmation, affection, and hugs from our families. These elements are *essential* to us, ensuring that we don't enter a marriage relationship feeling *deficient*. Because if we enter a relationship already deficient, we are more likely to fixate on what we are not getting out of the relationship.

And we'll miss the essence of what real love is.

If you didn't receive intentional care from your family of origin, I'm truly sorry. Thankfully, though, whatever you did or did not get from the family in which you were raised is not the end of the story. The psalmist wrote, "God places the lonely in families."[2] Friend, I'm not exaggerating when I say that God created the church to be a surrogate family to give you the love, affirmation, affection, and even hugs that you need so that you don't enter into dating, or marriage, deficient. God has the power to heal you, enabling your marriage to become what it is meant to be.

One way to care for your future spouse *right now*, as well as care for yourself, is to address the hurts you may still be carrying from the past:

If you battle depression or anxiety, address it and seek
wholeness.

If you struggle with insecurity, address it and seek wholeness.

If you have a crippling fear of rejection, address it and
seek wholeness.

If you haven't invited God to redeem your sexual history,
address it and seek wholeness.

If you have not healed from the abortion in which you
participated, address it and seek wholeness.

If you're dealing with a pornography addiction—you
guessed it: Address it and seek wholeness.

Real talk? A lot of what people label as "marriage" issues
are actually "singles" issues—issues related to experiences,
struggles, and failures from our single years! We bring baggage
into our marriages when we refuse to deal with the past. One
of the bravest and most impactful things you can do now to
prepare yourself for marriage in the future is ask for help.

Don't Be Bullied by Fear

"My mother caused my parents' divorce," Phil told me. "She
was always complaining—so much that my dad left."

Phil and I had been meeting together and talking about his
dating life—if you could call it that—when this came up.

I'd met young men like Phil before. They will only date
women who are passive. Women who don't have an opinion,
who won't speak up for themselves, and who only do what
they're told. In Phil's case, he believed if he could find a woman
who never complained, his future marriage would be less likely

to end in divorce. Even though his parents' divorce was certainly much more complicated than Phil's interpretation.

Phil was being bullied by fear. And there are a lot of people like him who are afraid that their next relationship, or their marriage, will end up like their parents'. Maybe it's because someone has a complaining spirit—and tongue!—but it may be something else.

> My dad controlled my mom. She never had a voice.
> They were always fighting with each other.
> My parents were married thirty-eight years, and I never saw them hold hands or hug.
> When my parents yelled at each other, I was terrified.
> I watched my dad beat on my mom.

A lot of people consider what they've seen at home and decide they don't want any part of it. And so they may choose not to date. Or they may date and not let people get too close. Or they may date with no intention of ever getting married.

Bottom line? They're afraid. And fear will never lead us to a good place. We're never going to win if our strategy is to run from what we don't want. From what we fear. The win comes from having a clear vision of what we do want. And when we deal with our fear of the past, we can finally walk into a healthy future.

There are plenty of reasons why fear can bully or dominate us. One of the letters Paul wrote to young Timothy assures him, and us, "God has not given us a spirit of fear, but of power and of love and of a sound mind."[3] And what that means is that we are given a new vision; we can look at what we've experienced with fresh eyes.

Maybe my parents' marriage was doomed because they
weren't submitted to God and didn't build their relationship on biblical principles.

Or maybe I did date someone who was dominating, but
God helps me understand why I did and how I can
avoid it next time.

Or perhaps I am scared of being in debt again, but God
wants to teach me how I can trust Him for what I
need—for what *we* need.

If you saw a car crash and decided to never drive a car
again, it would mean you're being dominated by fear. But instead, with a sound mind, you could also decide to learn from
why the car crash happened. Maybe the driver was texting and
driving. Maybe she was speeding. Maybe he was drinking.
And when you have that sound mind, you can choose to act
differently.

God can set you free from any fear that is bullying you.

Decide to Deal with the Baggage You Inherited from Your Family

Hear me: It's not just *you* who came from a crazy family. We all
did. We all came from families with mindsets that weren't biblical in some way, and maybe we've adopted dysfunctional be-
liefs. Then we bring those into our marriage.

Kevin grew up in a home where his financial needs were
not met. And, as a child, he vowed, "I'm never going to be
poor. I'm never going to look my kids in the eye and not be
able to give them what they need." There's nothing wrong
with working hard and providing for your family, but good

never comes from a motivation of fear and past pain. Kevin ended up neglecting his spouse and children—just so that he could make the money to provide for them.

Or you may have been brought up to believe that blood is thicker than marriage. So once you're married, you rush in to help when your siblings or parents get in any kind of trouble. You prioritize your original family above the new family unit God has given you. But what happens to your spouse or your children when you've used your money to pay a sibling's tuition? Or to help an extended family member with their mortgage? Or with their debt? And then your spouse doesn't agree with how you're spending your money, so you just make spending decisions on your own, and the next thing you know, you and your spouse have separate bank accounts. And when the money is separate, the heart separates, because the Bible says that "where your treasure is, there your heart will be also."[4]

I'm not at all saying you shouldn't help your parents or siblings, but when you leave your family of origin and cleave to your spouse, your priorities need to change.

Decide to Deal with the Baggage You Picked Up on the Journey

Sometimes we've gone through painful seasons. Maybe difficulty came as a result of poor decisions. Maybe it was just because we live in a sinful and fallen world, and pain has a way of finding us. Jesus taught that "in this world you will have trouble."[5] We *will* face challenges.

In Morgan's first serious dating relationship, during college, her boyfriend cheated on her. Rather than kick him to the curb, she chose to forgive him. When he did it again and pleaded with her to stay with him, she forgave him again.

Today, Morgan's in a relationship with a different man, which could potentially lead to marriage. But there's a problem. When her boyfriend is unavailable to her—because his phone is off or he's spending time with family or friends—she begins to lose it. She feels very anxious and insecure, and Morgan expresses her fear by lashing out at a man who's done *nothing wrong*. Morgan has not yet decided to seek healing from the hurt she endured as a young adult. And until she does, it will affect all of her relationships.

I don't know what it is for you. It might be something other than trust. You could be influenced by a past relationship with a man who abused substances, or one who took liberties with you sexually, or one who mistreated you in other ways.

You need to unpack your hurts before you date and marry, or it will be extremely difficult to experience what God has for you. I know this is difficult; facing the pain of life is such a daunting task. There is likely trauma in your past that you brushed off as "no big deal" because you didn't realize how much it would affect you. And then there are likely other past hurts you simply have no idea how to address, so it seems safer emotionally to avoid talking about them. Do not despair. God truly will guide, and I'm not just saying that. Start by journaling and unpacking what you've experienced. Naming your hurts and anxieties is the first step to disarming their power over you. Talk to a pastor or trusted leader at a church. Definitely consider talking to a licensed counselor. That may feel drastic, but it's not too extreme when the mission is finding wholeness.

If you're beginning to notice some hurts in your past or struggles in the present that you need to address, know this: God's got you. So let's look at some of the tools God uses to make you whole.

Q: Is it bad that I don't want to be married anytime soon?
A: Yes. However, if you don't plan to get married at all, I would say that's not bad, just make certain that is God's plan for your life and not a response to unhealed trauma. Assuming you are twenty-two or older, if you want to be married, but not soon, that's a massive problem. Proverbs 5:18 implies that your spouse should be found in your youth. Genesis 2:24 implies that the season you leave your parents' oversight is the same season you should be connecting to a spouse. Next to accepting Jesus as your Savior, marriage is the biggest decision you'll make, and the biggest decisions demand the most attention and preparation. You want to be able to build as much of your life as possible with an amazing spouse.

Q: What advice do you have for the single woman who is serving the Lord and still waiting for a mate?
A: All things are possible. I know people who have waited a long time and are now happily married and fulfilled. But I feel you. Finding a great mate is often more difficult than finding a needle in a haystack. So, you want your waiting to be extremely proactive. Examples of proactivity include: enlisting the help of close friends (married friends might be best) and spiritual leadership, using dating apps, being social and attending events, serving at your church, going to the gym, and so on. Don't expect God's best without using your faith. Faith is trusting that God will do what seems impossible. Fighting against discouragement and apathy is going to be an active and exhausting battle. You can do this.

Get a Tune-Up

Invite God to Make You Whole

WHILE A LOT OF PEOPLE TRADE IN THEIR CARS WHEN THEY HIT 100,000 miles, that wasn't the way my dad did it. He had Volvos that he'd drive for more than 300,000 miles. Once, he almost made it to 400,000! Yes, Volvos are good cars. But that wasn't his secret. The reason my dad's cars ran so long is because he never missed an oil change. When manufacturers recommend getting your oil changed every 5,000 miles or 7,000 miles, that is *not* just a suggestion. Because if you miss those oil changes, if you skip scheduling tune-ups, the engine of your car will fail long before the potential of the vehicle has expired. (If you didn't understand the significance of changing the oil until now, *you're welcome.*)

In Need of a Tune-Up

When Jessica was eight years old, an uncle touched her inappropriately. The first time he did it was while the rest of the family was watching football on Thanksgiving. The next time was when they were cleaning up the kitchen after Christmas dinner. Jessica explained to her older sister what happened, but her sister told her to just keep quiet.

In middle school, Jessica began to be sexually active with boys. She decided that she would do whatever she wanted with her body, and she did. Throughout high school and college, Jessica moved from boy to boy, from man to man.

Jessica met Christ through a campus ministry in college. When she began dating one of the leaders, Jonathan, they both committed to keeping their relationship pure. And one of the female staff members even guided Jessica through healing prayer to be released from her sinful past. So, when Jonathan proposed to Jessica, they began to look forward to the kind of physical relationship they'd share in marriage.

Both of them were surprised that on the night of their wedding, Jessica burst into tears the first time Jonathan touched her naked body. Jessica didn't know what was happening within her, and Jonathan certainly didn't either.

After engaging in prayer and fasting, speaking to her pastor, and spending time with a Christian therapist, Jessica slowly began to figure it out. While she *had* been forgiven and cleansed of the choices she'd made, she still needed to be set free from what had been done to her. Jonathan was patient as Jessica embraced that healing journey, but it did make their marriage more difficult in its earliest years. Without ever meaning to, we take our childhoods into dating and marriage.

Sometimes, we know the issues that we're dragging alongside us. While they may not surface for a minute, we're aware of what we're carrying. Maybe you suffered a wound of rejection from a parent, and you know that in your dating life, it makes you reticent to put yourself out there. Or perhaps your mother never knew *her* mother, so she didn't quite know how to nurture you. These kinds of experiences affect the way we do or don't care for others. For example, if you lost a sibling during childhood, you might be aware that such loss has an impact on the way you operate in relationships with others.

I have a friend I'll call John. And John leads a massive organization with thousands of employees. John was keenly aware of the childhood hurts he endured because he grew up in a home with an alcoholic father. As you may know, every person reacts differently to the early circumstances he or she faces. Another person who grew up in a similar home to John's might have also turned to drinking, but not John. Young John reasoned that while his father *lacked* self-control, he'd be different: He would *exercise* self-control. But John has vulnerably shared with me that the particular way he ended up dealing with his own childhood trauma was an overcorrection. Every strength has a weakness; it has a "shadow side." The way that hyper-self-control expressed itself in John's life caused its own set of problems.

Sometimes, we *don't* know the issues that we're dragging into dating. We don't see that the reason we don't want to go to football games with friends or out to the diner as a group is because there's a part of us that doesn't want to ever be in a position where we could be rejected. And so we don't even get close to members of the opposite sex. Or we may not realize that because we didn't receive emotional care from our parents, we don't know how to offer it to others. Or we reason that we were too young to have many memories of the older sibling who died, so it probably doesn't affect us much at all. Except that it does.

Unfortunately, even the hurts that we don't recognize, or don't acknowledge, *do* impact our relationships. Whether or not we realize it, our experience determines what we're looking for when we're dating. And that can be happening at a very primal level. For example, Patricia's father died when she was just eight years old. And part of her always hungered for the steadfast presence of a man who would take care of her. When Patricia was twenty, she started dating an older man. She learned that when he had gotten another young woman pregnant a few years earlier, he had provided an apartment for her and her baby. It was the kind of provision that Patricia's heart hungered for. Patricia became pregnant after just a few months of dating this man. And while she was completely unaware of what was going on inside of her at the time, years later, in therapy, she realized that while she certainly didn't get pregnant on purpose, a part of her longed to be provided for by a man.

Whether we're aware of the particular ways we've endured trauma or not, every one of us takes our childhood into dating. Since none of us were raised by perfect parents, we all leave our childhood homes with a few "bumps and bruises." If we haven't worked toward healing those old hurts, they will affect our dating relationships and, one day, our marriages. At *best,* they can make these relationships more difficult. At *worst,* they will destroy them. Even if we come from homes that look good, every one of us has to take responsibility for pursuing personal health.

You Can Heal

Although there is likely work to be done and healing to be pursued, there is hope!

I don't want to scare you into thinking that because of what you experienced as a child, you'll never be capable of a healthy relationship. I do, though, want you to pause and notice what does need to be healed inside of you to be your best self in a relationship—both for you and for your partner.

I am encouraging you to do the work to be made well. The degree of healing that's needed is proportional to the depth of the wound. Maybe you lived with a parent who prioritized work over family. You might have been bruised by that. Or maybe you were cruelly abused by someone who should have been protecting and nurturing you. That's a wound that runs deep.

Because I believe in God's power to transform, I have hope that you can be healed from the early hurts you suffered.

Take Your Heart to God

The first stop on the journey to pursuing personal health is your relationship with God. The first place to seek wholeness and wellness is in His Word. Carve out time to spend with God, feasting on His Word, speaking with Him, and listening for the message He is speaking to your heart. Perhaps you'll find a book or another resource that guides you on how to offer your hurting parts to God daily. Or maybe you'll carve out a spiritual retreat where you and God do some deep work in your heart. Ask God to show you how He wants to heal you.

Seek Counsel from Godly Mentors

The second stop on this journey toward health is a one-on-one pastoral relationship. Your dating life and future marriage depend on it. I'm serious. Don't play. If you aren't plugged in to a local church, now is the moment. Invest in a church community, and pursue pastoral counseling. Maybe that will be with the lead pastor. Maybe there is a pastor on staff who's uniquely equipped to offer counseling. Or there might be a layperson gifted in healing prayer who can journey with you. Through your local church, find the best person to travel with you as you move toward healing.

Pursue Professional Counseling

The third stop on your journey to being made well is professional counseling. Godly mentors are important, but many things we face need the insight of those who are specifically trained and certified to walk us toward healing. I encourage you to get recommendations from the staff at your church. Who, in your community, do they trust? Who do they recommend? When you seek care from a therapist, you're not abandoning the work you're doing individually with God. In fact, these professionals are often exactly the tool, the medic, that God can use to heal hurting hearts.

Consider Medication

And the fourth stop? It may be medication.

I know that in the past, this was a bit controversial in the Christian world. But the reason I *have* to put it out there is because I've seen individuals with levels of trauma so severe that they were not able to do the work—in those first three steps—to heal. The trauma had them paralyzed. So they needed medical interventions to enable them to do the work with God, the work with pastoral support, and the work with professional support. It was amazing to witness how receiving the necessary medication enabled these individuals to begin their journey toward healing.

While you might be eager to jump into a new relationship and reluctant to slow down for self-care, I encourage you to view this time spent on personal health as a valuable opportunity. This is the moment for you to get your house in order—so that you can flourish personally and so that you are ready to date.

Pursue Healing

Does any of this resonate with you? Notice the signs in your life.

Maybe you've seen the ways your early relationships have affected your subsequent friendships or dating relationships. You know you need help.

Or perhaps you don't have much dating experience but you recognize that there are hurts within you that need healing. You don't know why you burst into tears every Father's Day. Or you can't explain why you get all ornery and tank things, every year, on your birthday. Or maybe you recognize that snubs or missteps in friendships are harder for you to navigate than they are for others. You can read the signs.

I'm going to suggest, again, that the degree of healing you need is proportional to the depth of your wound. Before you take the next step in your dating journey, do the work you need to do to be made well.

Of all the options for healing I mentioned, your relationship with God is the most important. Seek wholeness and wellness in His Word. In prayer. With Him.

Doing the Work *Works*

Remember Jessica? With the support of her husband, she did all the things. She brought her wounds before God and asked the Spirit to guide her. She met with a pastoral counselor who was on staff at her church. That pastor suggested she work with a therapist who specialized in healing after sexual trauma. This therapist recognized signs of clinical depression in Jessica and referred her to a doctor who could prescribe the medication Jessica's body needed to do *good work*.

If you want to enter into marriage whole, do the work now. (Marriage aside, do the work to *be whole,* to be the person God made you to be.) God is so faithful to restore what has been broken. And He is with you in this.

You ready to hit the road? I've got something to say to the men, but first I want to help the women launch well.

Hit the Road, Women

Be Brave and Put Yourself Out There

Note: Hey, fellas, this chapter is for the ladies.
(I'd advise you to listen in.)

SHANIYAH, A TWENTY-NINE-YEAR-OLD GRAPHIC DESIGNER, REALLY wanted to be married. Ever since she was a girl, she'd dreamed of being a wife and a mother. Shaniyah worked from home, and when her workday ended, she'd treat herself to a good meal and then cuddle up on the couch and either grab a good book or binge *Suits* until bedtime. On the weekends, she might catch a movie with her girlfriends or worship on Sunday mornings, but that was the extent of her social interactions.

And Shaniyah, who was trusting God to bring her a husband, was still single.

The Bind

When women who are single seek counsel about dating, I hear the same refrains again and again:

> He should ask *me* out.
> I'm supposed to be *found*.
> I should be *pursued*.

More than one woman has asked me, "Should I be putting myself out there as a woman?" The answer is *yes*. One thousand percent yes.

The book of Proverbs announces, "A man who has friends must himself be friendly" (18:24, NKJV). To break it down: If you want friends, show yourself to be friendly. I'll be bold: You can't complain about being single, about not having options, about not having found the right person, if you're not willing to put yourself out there.

You have to be willing to take a risk.

And I understand the energy it takes. You may have to meet a few frogs before you find your prince.

A woman recently asked me if it's ever okay for the female to make the first move—to ask a guy out. I understand the reasoning behind her question. In the church, we've taken one little verse and created a whole doctrine around it: "A man who finds a wife finds a good thing."[1] You heard it, right? He's the finder. And she gets found.

While I think there are some good reasons that men should take the initiative to pursue women, I want us to think more broadly. Let's go bigger and get more creative. Let's look at some other passages.

You know the story of Ruth and her mother-in-law, Naomi? Tragically, Naomi lost her husband and both of her sons. And when she set off to return to her homeland, her daughter-in-law Ruth insisted on going with her. (Naomi couldn't shake her.) Well, when they got to the land of Naomi's birth, the two women had to figure out a new life for themselves there.

One of Naomi's kinfolk was named Boaz. And Boaz had it going on. One day, Naomi had an idea: She wanted Ruth to make herself "available" to Boaz. (Did that sound bad? It wasn't anything shady.) Ruth was game. Instructed by an older woman, Ruth made a move. Naomi told her to uncover that man's feet, and Ruth crept over to where he was sleeping and did it. She *literally* threw herself at his feet.

Now, I'm not saying you should run out and find your Boaz. He was a *lot* older than Ruth. And I'm definitely not telling you to go find a sugar daddy, but you get the idea. Naomi, the wiser mentor and guide, told Ruth how to put herself in the right place, at the right time, beside the right person. (We'll dish more about the wisdom of mentors in a later chapter.)

Being Available . . . and Drawing a Line

I actually don't think there's anything wrong with a woman making the first move.

Maybe you approach a man and introduce yourself.

Maybe you start up a conversation at a party.

Maybe you ask him to exchange numbers.

Maybe you invite him to join you and some of your friends at a movie or dinner.

You are making yourself available. You've let a guy know that you're interested. But then you give him the chance to step up.

Let him text you.

Let him call you.

Let him ask you out.

There's nothing wrong with putting yourself out there, but at a certain point—I'll suggest within the first three or four weeks of friendship—you need to draw a line and let him take some initiative.

Unfortunately, I've known some women who draw that line before they ever make themselves available. They'll say, "He needs to ask me for my number." "He needs to ask me out." "He needs to step to me." They draw the line *too soon*. The reality is that a lot of people, male and female, are socially awkward. They might be a little bit anxious. They might be introverts. They're not going to roll up to a stranger and start a relationship.

To be clear, I have no interest in throwing introverts under the bus. In fact, I am one. And here's the deal: Once the relationship is initiated, there's no one better at being genuine, at having deep conversations, at being transparent. So, if you draw that line too soon, you could be missing out on an intellectual, God-loving, affectionate, genuine person because you're expecting them to be an extrovert when God made them an introvert.

You may be saying, "Forget him; I'm the introvert. I'd rather voluntarily have a root canal than have to initiate a conversation with a guy I may be interested in." Like I said, I'm an introvert, so I absolutely get it, but I do want to challenge you. Personalities are not God-created prisons that we are unable to leave. You are going to have to step outside of your comfort zone at times to advance your vision for your life. This is one of those times.

I'm giving away my entire bag of tricks, but as an extreme introvert, I used to break the ice and initiate conversations by being active. Whether it's helping clean up after an event, studying with a group, working out, or something similar, activity forces natural communication and makes breaking the ice exponentially easier.

The Right Place

So let's talk a bit more about putting yourself in the "right place."

I hear a lot of single women saying that they haven't had a date in three years. But when I hear that, I'm going to ask what they've been doing for the last three years.

Have they joined a co-ed small group at church?

Do they join bike rides, go axe throwing, or participate in 5k runs in the community?

Are they hitting the diner with a group of female and male friends after worship night?

Are they willing to talk to the guy who speaks to them in the produce section at the grocery store?

If you haven't left your house in three years—yes, I'm absolutely throwing shade right now—how is anyone going to find you? If you're not on any dating apps, you only attend girls' brunches with your friends, and you serve on all-women teams at church, you probably shouldn't be surprised that you haven't been on a date in a while.

Sis, you gotta be like Ruth. You've got to put yourself where what you're looking for *is*.

I tell the ladies at our church all the time, "After the worship night on Friday, don't go home. Everybody's going out to so-and-so restaurant, like a dozen people. So go wait for your order to be screwed up, or forgotten, and stay out 'til one o'clock in the morning, laughing and joking." (You won't be able to do that when you're married with three kids—*trust me*—so now's the time.)

Put yourself *out there.*

I want you to be creative about finding new ways to be in the right place.

Maybe on a work trip, you strike up a conversation with someone you've only spoken to on the phone.

Or you might offer a cold water bottle from your pack to the guy on the running trail who really looks like he could use it.

Or you might even get really crazy and jump into the DMs of the dude at church who said he liked your car in the parking lot on Sunday.

Be intentional about showing up in the right places.

Elisha Knew What Was Up

In the Old Testament, there was a widow who was unable to pay her family's debts.[2] When the creditor was coming to take her sons as slaves to pay the debt, she cried out to Elisha. And God *showed up.*

All she had, she explained to Elisha, was a bit of oil. That was it. Now, to you, oil might not seem like much. But in the ancient Near East, it was a staple of the diet—used as an ingredient in bread and as a spread on top of it. It was used medicinally. It was used as fuel for lamps. It was used in religious offerings. It was used in international trade. You get it.

Well, Elisha instructed this woman to borrow all the empty jars from her neighbors that she could. Okay, whatever. Her marching orders were to pour the scant amount of oil she had into the borrowed jars. And as she did . . . every jar was filled! The woman was able to sell the oil and pay off the family's debts—and even live on what was left over.

You see where I'm going with this yet? (No, this widow is not about to get booed up with one of her neighbors who lent her the extra jars. Although, that's not out of the question.)

What I'm saying is that all she did was put out jars. And God filled them up.

For you, dating apps are one jar. Not the apps that are primarily known for hookups but the more serious ones.

Co-ed small groups at church are another jar.

Getting to the gym and being around other people is another jar.

Taking an improv class or going to game night could be another jar.

Signing up for a continuing ed writing class at the local college is another jar.

Volunteering at a local nonprofit is another jar.

Joel Osteen met his wife at a jewelry store.[3] And I mention that because we can get stuck on this idea that the only place you can find a spouse is in church. To be fair, that's a good place, but, sister, don't tell God where. Don't tell God how. Don't tell God who.

Put out jars.

You've got to give God something to work with. He'll do the miracle.

When We Refuse to Put Out Jars

It seems so simple, right? So why haven't you been putting out all the jars?

We just dished about the way that our old hurts can interfere with our relationships today. Well, when we haven't dealt
with the trauma in our past—especially when that trauma
planted a seed of *rejection*—we protect ourselves by refusing to
step into situations where we can be spurned.

Staying at home and binging Netflix every night? No one's
going to reject you.

Hanging in a tight group with just your girls? That's safe.

Recording TikTok dances by yourself every evening? You
won't get rejected.

Avoiding the kinds of situations where you could meet
men and maybe feel a little uncomfortable? You won't get
turned down.

You also won't be *chosen.*

If you want to find a spouse, you need to take a risk by
putting yourself out there.

Where Not to Put Your Jars

I don't think I need to tell you that there are places you don't
want to put your jars. You already know that you don't need
them piling up at home in your apartment where only you and
your cat are going to notice them. And at the same time, you
also don't need to be putting out too *many* jars by going on
countless dates. Neither approach is wise or strategic.

I'm also going to guess that, at some level, you know that
you're not going to bump up against a godly man in the club
on Saturday night. (Yes, God does miracles. But you've got to
give Him *something* to work with.) You're likely not going to
find the partner who's prepared to be a spouse in the club, at
the bar throwing them back, or at the hookah lounge. You

won't find him on that dating app you *know* is only for hook-ups. You know this.

But I want to go a little further and suggest that you want to pay attention to where you're dropping these jars *even at church.* (Wait, what did Pastor just say?) That's right.

A few months ago a woman at church told me that she was taking a break from dating for a season. She didn't want anything to do with guys. Her tone told me there was more to the story.

"Who have you been dating?" I asked.

This woman wasn't out at the club. She wasn't creeping around bars. She was at church.

Stay with me.

Not everyone who walks through the doors of a church on Sunday morning is equally invested, right? You've likely got your leaders—and I don't mean staff. I'm talking about people, staff or not, who are taking ownership in the church's ministries. Then you've got volunteers. They're serving in the nursery. They're showing up early to set up events. They're working. And then you've got members. They've joined, but they haven't really gotten serious, yet, about serving. Then you've got your visitors. Yes, they may be tall, strong, and handsome, but you don't always know where these folks are spiritually.

Well, this woman *had* been dating guys she'd met at church. But they weren't the leaders. They weren't the volunteers. Some were members who showed up. Others were visitors. And because they had technically walked through the doors, she'd met them "at church."

If you're dating someone who's not plugged into the life of the church, be cautious. I'll even go so far as to say that if someone isn't known by any leaders of the church, don't date them.

Yeah, I just said that.

You want to see fruit in the life of someone you're considering dating.

Other Places

Now that I said it, I don't want to find you creeping around the church office during the week just to scope out the interns and the volunteers and the staff. Settle down.

You can meet a really great guy at your friend's birthday party.

You can meet a godly man at a tech conference.

You can meet someone awesome at the library.

And here's a rule of thumb that's going to serve you well about *where* you meet someone: The less familiar you are with the space in which you meet someone, the more thorough you need to be about vetting them.

So if I meet you at a cookout at the home of my college roommate, there are people there who know you. We're not going on a date tomorrow, but I'm going to be less cautious in getting to know you. If we meet at an airport on the other side of the country and we hit it off over Chili's to go, I'm going to take it slow. I'm going to be careful. Because you don't have references. You could be a serial killer. I hope you're not, but you could be.

The less familiar the space in which I meet you is, the more cautious I'm going to be.

You Can Do This

Have you ever met a hardcore road tripper? They are *serious* about the journey.

One time, when I drove my brother to college, I wanted to be very intentional about avoiding DMV-area traffic as we left home in the morning. (District of Columbia, Maryland, and Virginia, if you don't know.) Oh, wait, did I mention that he didn't go to college in the D, the M, or the V? Nah, he went to school in Baton Rouge. Yeah, the one in Louisiana. So, we started our nineteen-hour trip at four in the morning. We did *not* play.

Sister, I know it takes courage to put out your jars. I am challenging you to be serious about this journey. I know you've got to put on your big-girl panties—that no one else is going to see until your wedding night—to put yourself out there and show up in the right places. But you can do this.

Guys, now it's time for you to hit the road.

Q: Should a woman make the first move?
A: Yes, if the first move is introducing yourself, asking him to hang out, or asking to exchange contact information. After that, a woman can ask a man to put a label, title, or definition on the relationship but should never ask him to be her boy-friend. Also, it's cool to ask him out once but never a second time. I don't have any issue with you initiating, but at some point early on, you've gotta let the man take the lead. Proverbs 18:22 says, "He who finds a wife." There is responsibility on the man to do the work to find and pursue. You can help him, but don't do it for him. Why? Because some great men are introverts, or even socially awkward, but ultimately a man values what he took initiative to do and who he pursued.

Hit the Road, Men

It's Time to Handle Your Business

Note: Ladies, this chapter is for the guys. (You are free to listen in.)

HAVE YOU HEARD THE STATS ABOUT INVESTING FOR RETIREMENT? This is solid intel, and I'm going to break it down for you.

If you begin putting away $100 a month at the age of twenty-five, you will accrue over a *million* dollars by the time you reach sixty-five. (Actually, $1,176,476 with a 12 percent rate of return, to be exact.) Only $100 a month, bruh. Now, stay with me. If you begin that process of setting aside money each month when you're thirty-five—the exact same $100— the value of that investment drops significantly. In fact, you will only accrue $349,496. (That's crazy, right?)

I want to say that the same is true of marriage: The earlier you start building your forever, the greater impact you and your wife can have—for each other, for your children, and for the legacy you were made to leave on this earth. The longer you wait, the harder it's going to be to build something great and lasting.

"I've Got Time"

If you're not yet actively pursuing a path to marriage—and maybe your sister or your auntie has got you reading this book—I want to name one of the traps that could be keeping you from doing so. The trap I've seen too many guys fall into is believing that they've got nothing but time. (If you're not this guy, I know you *know* this guy.)

As a man who cares about you, I want to sound the alarm: You don't have as much time as you think.

Now before you rush out to get booed up, first you need to have a plan for your life. In marriage, you're inviting a woman to join you in the mission God has for you, and if you don't have a plan *now*, that's going to be a problem. (I promise you that at least the women who are reading this book are going to have some serious questions for you.)

If you're getting to know a woman, and it's starting to go a bit deeper, you need to be prepared to honestly and thoughtfully answer these questions:

What are you passionate about?
Beyond making money, what do you want your life to be about?
What are the ways that God has uniquely gifted you?
What is God's calling on your life? What do you want to give your life to?

If you think the right answers are the standby "churchy" responses, I'll warn you that "God," "Jesus," and "Bible" ain't gonna cut it. When this woman asks you about the dreams you have for your life, what will you say?

You need to know the difference between a vision and a fantasy. A fantasy is something that you make up. It's something you want to accomplish because you believe it will make you look good or feel good. If it's a fantasy, you likely don't even know where to start. You don't have action steps. God hasn't given you the gifting to accomplish it. You might see the finish line *way in the distance,* but you don't know how you're going to get there.

When you have a vision, you not only see where you're going, but you know how to get there. You know what the first step is. The second step. The third step. In fact, you're already in motion. You're doing the work to align yourself with this vision day after day, month after month, year after year. And this vision aligns with the gifts that God has given you. You've sought out mentors who are guiding you—men who are living lives of impact and building their families, their careers, their ministries, and their legacies.

I don't want you thinking you have all the time in the world if you're not being intentional *today* about what you need to have in place before you pursue a wife.

"I've Got Options"

The second lie a lot of guys believe is that they have a lot of *options.* You may think you have lots of options, but let's look at that.

Yes, the ratio of women to men—in church and in the country as a whole—is in your favor. There are more of them, but not all of them are for you.

Some of the women you'll meet haven't yet done the work to become emotionally healthy.

Some may think they are ready for marriage but are not.

Some are recuperating from a toxic relationship and need time to heal.

Some may be looking for "intimacy" (sex) but have no desire for marriage.

Those aren't the woman you're looking for. The woman you're looking for is stable. She has dignity, character, and vision. She's ready to build forever with a guy who's ready for her.

The reason I want you to get started on this journey is because you may have to sift through a lot of bad matches before finding the one for you.

You're going to want to weed out the ones who "go to church" but aren't serious about their faith. You'll want to sift through those who are serial daters or have not fully committed to holiness. You'll want to move beyond the ones who are emotionally erratic and careless with their words. You'll want to go past the women who behave as if they're God's gift to humanity but are hiding deep insecurities behind their beauty, their success, their money, or their accomplishments.

This may surprise you, but you also want to look further than those who aren't bringing anything to the table *other than* their love for God. Don't get me wrong—I'm grateful for these women of the temple. These are the super spiritual women who think that they are so holy that even Jesus could learn a thing or two from them. But they need to grow in humility. They also need to bring more to the table than just their spirituality: conviction, opinions, vision, and strategy.

I know it sounds harsh, because no one's perfect. But dating and marriage are not ministry. They are not mission work.

You'll want to be intentional.

Guys, if you're not horrible, if you're a decent guy, you might have a lot of women hanging around you, making you *think* you have lots of options. Why would you choose to pursue one partner when you've got all these other women stroking your ego?

They're complimenting your threads.

They're cooking food for you.

They're letting you know they're praying for you.

They're cheering you on every time you post something stupid on social media.

They may be stroking your ego, but they're delaying your destiny.

Brother, be mature enough to step away from the fan club and look for the woman God has for you.

"I Don't Want to Be Rejected"

Maybe you're the guy with a lot of women around you. But maybe you're not that guy. You might be socially awkward. You might be an introvert, like me. While I never had a problem stepping up to a woman, there were times when I sure had to look in the mirror and give myself a pep talk.

"Man! If you don't ask her out this time, you're a punk!"

I'd make the move, but I really had to psych myself up first.

If this is you, you might just be scared. You may be afraid of rejection. You position yourself in hopes that a woman will make the first move, but you don't have the guts to step up.

I'm not saying you need to be bold enough to profess your love. During Bible study. Before y'all have ever spoken. Please . . . don't. You don't have to spell out interest, but I do want to encourage you to *show* interest through natural conversation. I'm simply saying that you need to step to her and start some normal conversations:

Hey, how you been?
How's your day been?
What's new in your life?
How's it going?
What are you excited about?
What are you passionate about?

Keep it casual. You got this.

Man to man, I do understand that you might be fearful. In fact, some guys who are scared will even hide behind their faith. They pretend to be so spiritually locked in on God that they don't have time for a relationship. If you really want to be married and you say you're too busy building your ministry, too busy praying and fasting, too busy reading God's Word, I am calling you out: You're scared. You may be struggling with insecurity. Or with lust. Or something else. Don't use your spirituality as an excuse not to confront your insecurities or fears.

You might not even realize you're hiding! You've just decided that one day God is going to drop a great woman in your lap. (That would be awesome, right?) But you need to get out there and find her.

Too often I've seen guys hide. Maybe you've seen it on TV or in the movies. A guy will be out with his boys at a bar or a club. There may be one alpha who's real outgoing and starts up a conversation with a group of women. By the end of the night, he can take his pick out of all the women. And the other guys in his crew? Maybe they get the leftovers.

Maybe.

While I don't assume that you're creeping around clubs to pick up women, I do think it can be tempting to stay with your boys in a group. So whether it's in the church lobby after service or at a Super Bowl party with other singles, make sure you break off from your guys. Initiate a conversation with one woman without the protection of your homies.

Just Do It

Bruh, what are you waiting for?

I've heard stories about men who had planned to see the world. When they were young, they imagined themselves traveling to Chicago and Paris and Cape Town. But instead of making it happen, they worked. And they worked. And they worked. And when they finally "got around to it," their circumstances or their health had changed, and they never took those trips.

Don't wait.

Whether you're the guy who's shy and awkward around women or the one with looks, a degree, success, money, and charisma—the time to handle your business is now. You're not looking for a woman who is perfect, but instead you're looking for someone who is a perfect match for you. A partner who complements the gifting and calling and anointing God has put on your life. You're looking for a woman who will help you grow, and that quality can only be *found*—not attracted.

Brother, don't play. Don't wait. Don't hide. Don't fear. Right now, begin building a life worth joining. And then step up and make your move.

Now that you're in motion, I'm fixin' to point out the obstacles you'll want to avoid.

Nicknames for Yo' Boo Thang

1. Bae
2. Boo
3. Baby
4. Mine
5. Wifey
6. Sweetie/Sweetie pie
7. Pooh
8. Muffin
9. Love
10. Honey

Avoid These Obstacles

Steer Around Roadkill and Other Roadside Hazards

WHEN I WAS A KID, MY FAMILY WAS DRIVING HOME FROM NEW Jersey on I-95 when our car struck a metal pipe lying in the road. The impact punctured our radiator, causing all the fluid to quickly drain out. That pipe put us hours behind schedule that night. And while I wasn't even old enough to drive yet, I learned something about hazards on the road: *Avoid them if you can*.

Making a List and Checking It Twice

I'll bet you've seen a rom-com or two where the single woman, or single guy, has made a list of what they want to find in a mate.

And maybe you have too. Whether you've written it in the private pages of your journal or hidden it in your heart, I know there's something—or maybe a lot of somethings—you'd like to find in the person you hope to marry. And while I'm asking you to be intentional about this journey you're on, if you've made a fifty-point list of the qualifications of the "perfect" spouse for you, that list can be as dangerous as a stray pipe on the highway! It really does have the potential to cause some serious delays.

I've read some of these lists, so I'm just going to break the ice and put a few out there.

Her List: What She Wants in a Man

Maybe you haven't put your list online. Maybe you've only shared it with your BFF. But I know you got a list . . .

He writes poetry.
He makes over $100K.
He's 6'4" and 227 pounds of chiseled steel.
He's got delicious mocha skin.
He's got a neat fade or soft flowing hair.
He's sensitive.
He fasts seven days every month.
He has no debt.
He owns his own home.
He drives a Mercedes.
He brings me flowers every time he sees me.
He comes from a healthy, intact family.

I'm not saying these are *bad* things. They're not. But there is a good chance the person you marry may be a truly wonderful, godly person who will only tick . . . like . . . *two or three* of these boxes.

His List: What He Wants in a Woman

Brother, I know you're not putting this list in a journal where your homey can find it and humiliate you. But I know you got a list . . .

She has the body of a Kardashian.

She has long hair.
Naturally beautiful, she looks the same with or without makeup.
She's a well-networked influencer.
She comes from money.
She's building her career now but wants to stay home with kids.
She wants to be around me when I want to see her but is totally cool when I hang with my boys.
She's confident and has strong opinions but is also submissive and will never disagree with me. (Basically, she's a submissive boss chick.)
She's never dated anyone before me.

I'm not saying these are bad things. They're not. But the person you marry will have . . . like . . . *two or three* of these qualities and is still exactly who God has for you.

Ladies, I would not be surprised if you have a list so detailed that you wouldn't even date Jesus. My guys, your list, even if just mentally recorded, is probably way too detailed as well.

Being Too Picky

When you've got an elaborate list that no human being can live up to, you're creating an *obstacle* for yourself on this dating journey. Now, when it comes to dating, I want you to be picky as you're hunting for a spouse, but I don't want you to be *too* picky.

What's too picky?

I won't date anyone who doesn't have a four-year degree.
I won't date a man who can't quote Bible verses from memory, because he has to lead me spiritually.
I won't date a woman who doesn't speak in tongues.
I won't date anyone who can't cook.
I won't date anyone who doesn't keep their house consistently clean.
I won't date anyone who has children.
I won't date anyone from *that* fraternity.
I won't date anyone from *that* sorority.
I won't date any girl who didn't play sports in high school.
I won't date anyone who does not honor Queen B as the pop goddess she is.

If you choose to be *that picky,* you may be missing out. You won't do yourself any favors with your unwieldy, unrealistic list.

In fact, I'll keep it real: It's possible that you're looking for a mythical creature. If you've been looking for Mr. Right or Mrs. Right, you may have your sights set on someone who doesn't exist.

He just gets me.
We have chemistry.
It doesn't feel forced or orchestrated.
It was meant to be.

She accepts me with all my flaws and issues.

He makes me feel complete.

This person makes the pain of my past disappear.

So are you looking for a mythical creature? You might be.

The "Right" Person

So let's talk about who the "right" person is for you.

The right person is not someone who was made specifi-cally for you—as you are now. The right person is made for the best version of you. That's certainly true in my case. My wife was made for the best version of me. She isn't the best fit for who I was when we were friends, or maybe even who I am today. She's the best fit for who God created me to be. She was made for the whole me. She's made for the person I'm grow-ing into.

The reason you want to be *very intentional* about your "right person" is that if you marry, you're doing a really ambi-tious thing. You are choosing to spend your life with someone and build something that has never been built before, all while taking fire from the Enemy. So who you are building with—who's fighting next to you—is a pretty big deal. Probably a bigger deal than whether he is 6′4″, has mocha skin, and writes poetry. A bigger deal than whether she is 5′5″, looks like a goddess, and loves Xbox. (By the way, neither one exists.)

So if you're willing to let go of your list, I want you to begin imagining the *type* of man or woman you want to build a lasting marriage with.

As you open yourself up to finding this person, I want to caution you not to over-spiritualize it by limiting it to things like:

I need a word from God.

I won't get coffee with her until I hear from the Lord.

I'm waiting on biblical confirmation before we grab
lunch.

I need a prophecy from God in order to speak on the
phone with him.

I was already a senior pastor before I was dating seriously.
And some of those girls out there in the church world thought
they were impressing me with how spiritual they were.

"I'm going to go on a forty-day fast to determine if I
should be your girlfriend," one announced.

"Don't bother," I offered. "I won't be around thirty days
from now."

I'm not throwing shade, but you know it's too much. It's
not like I was proposing marriage. If I asked a girl out, it was
because I was interested in getting to know the real her.

When we over-spiritualize dating, when we go too deep
too soon, we may miss out on the great guy, or the great girl,
who wants to get to know us over a cup of coffee.

You Can't Change People

Okay, I've got another roadside hazard that you want to avoid.

Too often I find people dating someone who they don't
agree with. They're not heading the same way in life, but
they're waiting for, and expecting, the other person to change.

Uh . . . *no.*

In my freshman year of college, I was interested in somebody, and it just wasn't the right person. And you know how
everybody else knows they're not the right person, but you're
trying to be hardheaded and ignore the obvious? My parents

were so gracious. They just kept checking in. I won't lie: I used to think that my mom wasn't that bright. But now I'm realizing my mom's smarter than I ever knew. About that time, she was just talking —not even about dating—and she said something that scared me like nothing else.

She said, "Stephen, you know, I'm pretty much the same woman I was when I was sixteen." Then she added, "Yeah, I've matured a little bit. I'm following Christ now, but my personality and my temperament and all were pretty much set." And you know what she was really telling me? "Stephen, that girl ain't going to change." (You know I dumped the woman I was dating the next week, right?)

My mom was a freakin' genius. She tricked me into doing what needed to be done.

We expect people to conform and transform and contort to fit into our lives. We want that. We hope for it. But what we need to do is to call a spade a spade. We need to name the fact that we are not heading the same direction.

It's not your job to change people. You don't have that ability. God refuses to control people, so why do we think we can? We try to fit people into our boxes and our expectations instead of letting them be them.

It's better to go your separate ways than think you can change someone.

Thanks, Mom.

What About Love?

Let's look at another wily obstacle to avoid when dating.

Our culture has told you that love is an emotion. Society, Hollywood, and your bestie have convinced you that love is about how you *feel*. And if you just find the right person, you can fall in love and live happily ever after.

The problem is that the assignment to "find the right person" sets us up to believe that there's a perfect person.

There's not.

One woman who set out on a hunt for that perfect person, for that "soulmate," is Brittany Renner. Brittany is a social media superstar, actress, fitness model, author, app developer, and Instagram influencer. In fact, Coach Deion Sanders at the University of Colorado brought her in to speak to his players about how women like her survey and trap athletes who have the potential to make a lot of money. Ms. Renner is best known for her fitness and Instagram exploits.

Let's slow our roll and pause right there at "exploits."

Ms. Renner has been with *a number* of NFL and NBA players. She was out there trying to find her *soulmate*. And while, by worldly standards, Brittany's body count is "impressive," she admitted, "I know what it's like to be desired by men. I don't know what it's like to be *valued* by one."[1]

While her past is marked by her sexual "exploits," today Renner is singing a different tune. She explains, "It's disgusting. I hate even having that spiritual tie [to the men I slept with] in any type of way."[2]

One of the messages we hear is that love is about how we feel. And there's this objective soulmate for us out there. When we find that person, we'll have all the feels *forever*. But that lie is setting us up for harm. Love is not at all about what we feel. It's about so much more.

God Knows

Clearly, I think that looking for a soulmate is problematic.

We can get messed up in the church, in a sort of mind game, when we go down the rabbit hole of "destiny" and "God has a plan" and "He knows the end of a thing from the beginning of a thing." That sounds a lot like a "soulmate" to me. And while it's true that God does know who you're going to marry before you ever meet that person, I need you to hear that when you meet them, *they will not be perfect.*

It's naïve to think that there is only one person who's going to check all, or even most, of the boxes on your list.

Do I think you should have a list? Well, it depends on what you include. Yes, there are qualities to look for, but, no, you're not helping yourself if the person you're looking for has to check off twenty boxes. When we lay out those boxes, it's like we're putting God in a box. We've got a limited view of what He has called us to do. We've limited who God might bring our way. There are certainly nonnegotiables; a potential spouse must be actively seeking to grow in Christ, be kind, and have integrity. But these are boxes hundreds of thousands of people tick.

Let the list of twenty criteria go. Crumple it up, and throw it in the trash.

Attraction

But let's get honest about attraction. It matters. Let's not get so spiritual that we act like God did not give us attraction. The person God has for you is going to be someone you're drawn to. We've just got to make sure that physical attraction isn't our only decision-making factor. Deep attraction can easily cloud our thinking. There will be people you are very attracted to who *aren't* God's best for you. To keep it real, the person you're attracted to, the one who's your exact "type," might not be the one God has for you. (I know, I know, that might feel disappointing.) But when we're attracted to a type, especially when that type doesn't line up with what's most important to God, it might be coming from a place in us that's broken. That's real, friend.

Be careful about being guided by attraction and by your feelings.

Recently someone asked me what I thought about "falling in love." And it felt like maybe they were trying to corner me, since they know that I'm coming at dating and marriage in a pretty practical way. I think that my answer surprised them.

"I believe that falling in love is real."

Surprise!

"But," I added, "you need to understand that you could also fall *out* of love."

You need to realize that you could fall in love with the wrong person. And you could fall *out* of love with the right person.

The Bible says that where your treasure is, there your heart is.[3] We often think that's only talking about money, but our greatest treasure is our time. We've only got sixty minutes in every hour, twenty-four hours in every day. If someone invests time in a person, they are going to develop feelings for them. So, yeah, a man falls in love with his wife. But if that's the measure, he can also fall in love with his secretary. Yes, falling in love is real.

So we want to step back and ask, "Did I invest enough time, and learn enough about a person, that my heart did what the Bible says my heart is gonna do?" Ask if you've developed affection for, empathy with, dreams of a God-glorifying life with the person you've fallen in love with (whether it's your future wife, co-worker, or opposite-sex bestie).

That's why I don't want you to think falling in love is confirmation that someone is the person God has for you. Because after you choose a spouse that way, you can just as easily fall out of love with your wife and fall in love with the nurse at your doctor's office. Guess what? After you marry *her*, you're going to fall out of love with her. And you're going to fall in love with the next person. The problem with this "falling in love" logic is the mindset that whoever you happen to have affection for is who you should spend the rest of your life with.

Nah.

Avoid Roadside Hazards

Maybe you've never been really intentional about how you determine the person with whom you want to spend your life. But now you know that there are roadside hazards you can avoid:

- Don't cling to your thirty-point checklist of who your future spouse needs to be.
- Don't be too picky and miss out on someone great.
- Don't over-spiritualize the whole process.
- Don't plan on changing anyone.
- Don't trust ooey-gooey emotions to guide you.

And now that you know what to avoid, let's look at how you can find—and be!—the type of person you're looking for.

What is love bombing? At the beginning of a relationship, someone may "bomb" you with affection. They may be extremely complimentary, constantly telling you how wonderful you are. They might shower you with gifts. They may be eager for your time and attention. They could communicate their love for you very transparently. Ultimately, though, their posture becomes manipulative and possibly even abusive.

 What is gaslighting? Gaslighting is the way someone psychologically manipulates their partner. This person may question your memory of events, saying, "I think you're forgetting what really happened." They might make you question your own legitimate needs, claiming, "You're too needy and clingy." This person might twist the meaning of love, insisting, "I'm only doing this because I love you." Gaslighting causes you to question your own perception of reality.

 What is benching? Benching is when a dater will put someone "on the bench"—saving them for later—while they explore other options and look for someone better.

Trust the Guardrails

What to Look for in a Mate

IN THE BEGINNING, GOD LOOKED AT ADAM AND SAID, "THIS IS not good."[1]

Specifically, it wasn't good that Adam was alone. Now, I don't know if Adam had eaten the same meal twenty-one days in a row or if he was running with scissors. I don't know what happened, but we know that brother needed a woman. And God was going to help him out. It wasn't good that Adam was alone.

Next to having a relationship with God, marriage is one of the major relationships God designed us for. While not everyone is called to marriage, I am guessing that doesn't describe you or you wouldn't have made it this far in this book. If you want to find the right person to marry, you need to be intentional. And as you've got your eyes open for your partner, the one God will give you so that you're not alone, there are certain guardrails that can protect you from getting attached to someone who is *not* for you.

Guardrail #1: Only Date Someone Who Has Demonstrated They Have a Real Relationship with God

Sandra met David on a dating app a friend had met her husband on. She'd been really careful about only engaging in conversations with guys who said they were Christians. And she had really enjoyed the two dates she'd had with David.

A few days after that second date, David texted, "So how open are you to spending the night?"

Sandra was shocked. *Wait, didn't he say he was a Christian?*

I may not have to tell you this, but nine out of ten—no, ninety-nine out of one hundred!—people who check the "Christian" box on their dating profile are not submitted to the things of God. They checked that box either because they've been to church a few times or because they want to get a "good" woman.

Here's the real: Finding the person you want to spend the rest of your life with is like finding a needle in a haystack. It may be like it was for Sandra's friend—that one profile out of two thousand on an app. Or it may be that one guy out of the seventeen who go to your church—despite the three hundred other women who are going after those seventeen guys. The reality is, it's a needle in a haystack. Don't let one person who was untruthful about being submitted to God discourage you from giving God room to move.

That said, be smart. If you see someone attractive and

they've checked the box, you may *want* to believe that they're good to go. But without evidence, you don't know that. Look for *evidence* in a person's life of one thing: God is able to speak to that person about something in their life, and that person is able to hear it and receive it and allow God to change them.

If you get married, you can know with 100 percent certainty that you are going to marry a flawed human. And you can also know with 100 percent certainty that you do not have the ability to change that person. So, the only way to guarantee that my spouse's flaws are not going to bankrupt my life is if my spouse is submitted to the One who is able to change them—God.

You *have* to see that before you marry someone.

I don't care how cute they are.

I don't care how rich they are.

I don't care if they can finish your sentences.

I don't care how much your heart goes pitter-patter when they walk by. (The heart is deceitful above all else according to Jeremiah 17:9. Word?)

You have to see that this person is submitted to God. If God wants to speak to them about their anger, they can hear Him. If God challenges this person on a bad habit, they receive that word and work toward change. If God wants them to forgive a parent who failed, this person is softhearted enough to accept that word and strong enough to be obedient.

Above all, look for someone who is submitted to God.

Once you're married, there are going to be countless issues on which you disagree that you will not see when you're dating. You just won't. No one's trying to fool the other, but everyone is on their best behavior. Trust.

I'm thinking of a couple with differing political opinions. We'll call them Joe and Janise. He's a staunch Republican, and she's a die-hard Democrat. Now if either one is sold out, giving 100 percent of their allegiance to a political party, we've already got a problem. (I'm going to say that Republicans are missing 50 percent of the Bible, and Democrats are missing 50 percent of the Bible.) If either spouse's allegiance is to a political party, that's trouble.

But two spouses with differing opinions on politics, social views, or any other issue—*when they're both submitted to Jesus*? That can work.

(Will some couples need to agree not to discuss politics? Yes. If they want to stay married, yes, they will.)

No matter what you agree on or don't agree on, you want to be with someone who, at the end of the day, is submitted to Jesus. Someone who is teachable. Correctable. Open to being transformed by God.

If you meet a guy or girl on the bus, at the grocery store, or on a hiking trail, and you don't know if they have a relationship with God, don't go out with them. Don't get dinner. Don't get coffee right away. Take it slow. Because you may fall in love with the wrong person. When you invest enough time, you can fall in love with someone you do *not* want to end up with. Don't assume you're mature enough to date someone you're unsure about without catching feels. You're only fooling yourself.

Guardrail #2: Find Someone Whose Strengths Complement Yours

When my friend Trina met the man who would become her husband, her first reaction was, "He's not my type." Trina knew exactly what type of man she liked. She knew who she was attracted to. But that wasn't the man she *needed*.

Can I get an amen?

The first time you meet the person you'll marry, you might hate them. Okay, *hate* is strong. Maybe a better way to say it is you might be turned off.

Trina is a corporate boss, running a multimillion-dollar organization. And she was used to dating guys who were also very assertive. But what she was used to was not what God had for her based on the way He made her.

And it's the same for men who have a type. My friend Andy, nearing forty years old, has a net worth of about ten million dollars. He owns a residential construction company and is doing all right for himself. And Andy is looking for some boss chick who looks good on Instagram. He can see it in his mind: "When we walk into a room, we look good. She's got her business; I've got my business. She's rich; I'm rich."

"Dude, who's gonna pay attention to the kids?" I asked him.

I'm not saying that he can't find a woman who's been successful in her career, but I am saying that partners in a marriage are made to *complement* one another. They do not need to be mirror images of one another.

The person God has for you may not be who you expect. And they'll likely be different, in various ways, than you.

Don't look for a mirror image of yourself. If you're on the fast track professionally, your partner doesn't have to be. If you're extremely sensitive, the right partner for you might be someone who makes decisions from a more logical and rational place. If you're an introvert, your partner might be more extroverted. God is going to build something through your marriage one day, and your union, your family, will benefit when you each bring different gifts and strengths to the relationship.

Guardrail #3: To Find the Right Person, Be the Right Person

You already know what the Hollywood version of finding the right person is, don't you? You date the "right person," you "fall in love," and you put all your hopes and dreams into that person—until they don't work out anymore. Then you break up and go find another "right person." And when you find that "right person," you "fall in love" with them and put all your hopes and dreams there. And when that doesn't work out, you go and find the next "right person."

Without even realizing it, you're training yourself for divorce. Because you've taught yourself to identify the right person as whoever *feels* like the right person. You fall in love until you fall out of love. You fix all your hopes and dreams on someone who was never designed by God to fulfill them, which guarantees failure.

The world will tell you to spend all your energy looking for the perfect partner, so we're often just searching, searching, searching for the right person. Stop looking for the right person and *pivot*. Shift your energy. Instead *become* the right person.

You will only find the right person when you make it your mission to be the right person. You can trust that if you handle what God has called you to handle, He will take care of the rest.

You become the right person when you submit your life to God and look to Him to transform you. You become the right person as you grow in your relationship with God.

Focus on your side of the street. Handle your business and offer your wounded places to God for healing.

You become the right person when you love and serve the people around you.

Stop looking. *Become.*

When I encourage you to *become* the right person—rather than put all your energy into finding the right person—that's a double blessing. Yes, it's going to benefit your future marriage. But every single day between this moment and the day you walk down the aisle, you are going to benefit from investing time, energy, and maybe even dollars into becoming the person God made you to be.

Use the Guardrails

When I was in college, I drove for my father's medical courier company. That meant I was on the road for five hours a day, Monday through Friday. On one of those days, I was beat and struggled to stay awake. When I couldn't keep my eyes open for one more minute, I dozed off and awoke to the sound of my car ramming into one of those orange construction barriers, shattering the side-view mirror on my car. But you know what? I didn't slide off the road.

Just like those bumpers kids use when they're bowling, guardrails are there to keep you from falling in the gutter. Watch for them. Respect them.

There is no guarantee that the next person you are interested in or start dating will ultimately be the person you marry. However, you greatly increase that probability if you remain within the safety of wise parameters rather than giving everyone and anyone a chance.

Look for evidence that this person is submitted to God.

Find someone whose strengths are different than yours.

Become the right person.

Trust the guardrails.

The way that you choose to navigate singleness will determine your readiness to enjoy a satisfying, intimate relationship with your spouse. (You guessed it. We're fixin' to talk about sex. I know you're not going to put this book down right now . . .)

Follow the Rules of the Road

―――――

How to Live Right While Living Single

IF THERE'S AN EXCUSE FOR HAVING SEX BEFORE MARRIAGE, BELIEVE me, I've heard it.

> But we love each other.
> We know we're going to get married.
> We're adults.
> We weren't virgins anyway—it's not like it was our first
>   time.
> God will forgive us.
> God knows our hearts.
> I know Christians who had sex before marriage, and
>   when they got married, it worked out.

And not only do I want to push back on all of these excuses, but I also want you to know why I'm not buying them.

First and foremost, whenever we disobey God, it interrupts our relationship with Him. Some of us are so desperate to date somebody that we'll abandon our relationship with God for a physical relationship with an attractive person.

Second, just because a couple ends up married doesn't mean it "worked out." A lot of people have sex before marriage, get married, and then one partner commits infidelity. And the other partner is shocked. Appalled. They think, *How could someone who loves me do this to me?* Well, in a way, their partner was already operating in that mode. They never had a season where they proved they could control their sexual desires. They became accustomed to being intimate with someone they were not married to. They have always believed that intimacy does not require long-term commitment. They already have experience sleeping with someone they're not married to.

God's good intention for sex is that it would be the glue within marriage that bonds a couple in a very particular way. But some who've had sex before marriage will discover that once they get married there's not the same level of excitement, intrigue, danger. They miss the thrill of breaking the rules, so they seek out an experience to regain the same rush. But where there's sin, we know there's guilt and shame. And where there's guilt and shame, there's the temptation to avoid God. What many people do not stop to calculate, while dating, is that the choices we make *before* marriage impact our experience *of* marriage.

Having sex before marriage impairs your ability to make sober decisions. Remember that one reason God created sex is to bond a married couple together supernaturally. That is where we get the idea of a "soul tie" from. If you are bonded to someone sexually, you are less likely to see red flags. You will overlook the fact that they are really bad with money and struggle to remain employed. You are less likely to see that their outbursts of anger or demeaning comments are a habit and not just something that comes out on rare occasions. Sex can keep the wisest and most rational hypnotized—blind to behaviors that are cause for concern in the person they are dating.

I was visiting New York City a few years back. Traffic there is crazy. I was walking down a one-way street when I saw a car turn onto the street *going the wrong direction*. I mean, this wasn't a wrong turn in the middle of nowhere. It was Manhattan! And that error almost cost the driver their life. The rules of the road are rules for a reason. They equip you to reach your destination safe and sound. And I want to say that the rules God has established for our sexuality—in singleness, dating, and marriage—equip us to reach our destination safe and sound.

One of the biggest struggles you'll face when you're dating is sexual temptation. But with God's help, you can navigate dating and stay faithful to God in the process. I want to offer you a mini road map for how—and why!—to live *pure* in these days when you are trusting God to bring you a spouse but they've not yet shown up.

1. Exercise Good Boundaries
with People You're *Not* Dating

Some of the people I dated? Today they don't want anything to do with me. And that's because when I broke it off I was clear:

"Don't call me. Don't text me. No, we can't just hang out. You're not dead to me, but we're breaking up for a reason. Lose my number."

I know, that's a lot. I promise you I wasn't being a jerk. Okay, maybe just a little. I didn't say it quite like that, but I believe being unclear is unkind. When you leave the door open with an ex who you really don't see a future with, you are leading them on and being hurtful. Remember that those we date are made in the image of God and therefore deserving of our highest respect.

You don't need to have friendships with your exes. Because, sure, you might intend to be friends. But then someone catches feels again. And you're so intimately tied to them— whether the relationship was a godly one or an ungodly one— that it gets really complicated.

Cut. It. Off.

Because guess what? When someone who might actually be a good match comes around, they're going to pay attention to how you are behaving around your ex. And if the two of you are out at late hours, laughing at each other's jokes, and texting nonstop, it's going to be really confusing and, likely, off-putting for the person who's watching you.

Can you be cordial? Sure.

Can you be polite? Of course.

But you don't need to be BFFs.

Now, is friendship with an ex different than regular friendship with another person of the opposite sex? Yes. Yes. Yes. You're still going to exercise healthy boundaries in your friendships, but the boundary—the *wall*—needs to be much sturdier with an ex.

You win at living single when you're smart about exercising healthy boundaries with those you are *not* dating.

2. Exercise Good Boundaries
with the Person You're Dating

Not long after Trey and Chivon began dating, each quietly began to wonder if they'd found "the one." Both had saved themselves for marriage, and it seemed they'd found their person. Within three weeks, their relationship had gone deep. While they remained pure sexually, they knew how much money each other made. They knew the deep secrets of each other's family. They knew how many children they wanted to have together. It was quick; it was exciting. But when they broke up two months later, it was devastating for them both.

I want to suggest that exercising healthy boundaries as a single person applies to more than "just" sex. Boundaries apply to all aspects of intimacy. True intimacy with someone is revealing the deepest parts of who you are. If you are only weeks or months into a new relationship and you are already making plans for your future together, you may want to reconsider. Perhaps you are revealing too much too soon. Discussing how much money you make, how many kids you want (if any), what trauma you experienced, and what your sexual preferences are exposes your heart in ways that will leave you devastated if the relationship doesn't work out.

Even if it does work out, having these discussions too early can create a rescuer or victim dynamic in your relationship instead of promoting an atmosphere of partnership and mutual respect. You may feel obligated to protect the person you are getting to know after learning all they have been through. Or you may view this person as the missing piece to the puzzle of life that you are trying to build. This level of intimacy may have you committing to a mission or goal and missing the actual person and who God designed them to be apart from all they have experienced.

When you're single, whether you're dating or spending time with a friend of the opposite sex, be smart about *all* the boundaries you set up around your relationship, not just sexual ones.

When you are dating someone, I would strongly encourage you not to be alone in a private space like a dorm room or apartment. When you start kissing, and then French kissing, you are wired to take those acts to completion. I remember feeling so annoyed every time I was at Zai's house when we were dating and her mother would leave to work her night shift; her departure meant it was time for me to leave too. I was an adult who loved God and was already a pastor, but I also needed to respect Zai and not put myself in a position where I might be tempted to take things too far.

Exercise healthy boundaries out of respect for your future spouse, out of respect for yourself, and ultimately out of respect for the Lord who loves you and knows what's best for you.

You win at living single when you're smart about exercising healthy boundaries with the woman or man you are dating.

3. Avoid Sexual Sin for *Your* Sake

You already know that when you're single, the Enemy gives you endless excuses for why you should seek sexual gratification outside of marriage.

This is the twenty-first century.
Everyone is doing it.

It's not a big deal.

It's your body and your decision.

You love this person.

You two will get married eventually.

And those statements are just low-hanging fruit. The devil will suggest many more. But I need you to hear that if you entertain the Enemy's foolishness—rationalizing sinful choices—you are setting yourself up for trouble.

When you're single, you are under attack. But also, marriage is not a cure-all for what ails you. Because when you are married, you are also under attack. Both before and after marriage, one of the Enemy's primary goals is to get you to sleep with someone you are not married to. When you choose to follow God's plan *before* marriage, you're actually making an investment in your eventual marriage.

But today, as you're trying to live faithfully in your singleness, I want you to avoid sexual sin for your own sake. When you sin with your body, you sin against God. And sexual sin damages your relationship with God. Your stubborn refusal to live God's way makes it harder to hear God's voice in other areas as well.

You win at living single, and you preserve your relationship with God, when you avoid sexual sin.

4. Avoid Sexual Sin So That You Can Be Clearheaded About the Person You're Dating

When we're dating, we're just learning who the other person is. We're investing time. We're seeking to determine if this is someone we vibe with just as a friend or if this is someone we were made for. And when we jump into bed before that has even been determined, we don't have the chance to know who we're dealing with. Having sex with someone causes you to put up with behaviors you wouldn't otherwise put up with in the other person. When you're sleeping with someone, you're going to overlook some of the yellow and red flags that you'd otherwise be clearheaded enough to see. You won't know if this is the person God has for you if your judgment is cloudy.

You win at living single, and preserve wise discernment about the person you're dating, when you avoid sexual sin.

5. Avoid Sexual Sin for the Sake of Your Eventual Marriage

You already *know* what the Bible says. You *know* what the culture says. But I want to challenge you to consider the real-life consequences of deciding to sleep with someone before marriage. And if you've already made this decision, I need you to hear clearly that God redeems and God is inviting you to begin living well *today.*

One of the reasons it's important to be patient, to control yourself before you get married, is because dating is the training ground for marriage. If you don't train yourself not to be governed by your emotions before you say "I do," then—without a revival from God—you will not be able to control yourself after you say "I do." Whether you are a man or a woman, when you're dating, you commit to loving well by practicing patience and self-control: "I'm going to make a decision to love you by practicing restraint even if my emotions are telling me to hurry up."

Here's the bottom line: Sex before marriage is going to ruin dating, and it can also threaten your eventual marriage.

Sex before marriage affects your relationship with your future spouse—whether you marry the person with whom you're having sex or someone else. When you're having sex outside of marriage, you're practicing sleeping with someone you're not married to. So you've spent all this time practicing sleeping with people, and then once you are married, your desire is for something you're now not allowed to engage in. I think we can agree that infidelity is never okay; when we are sleeping with people before we get married, it's like we're in training for unfaithfulness in marriage.

"I don't know what happened! After we got married, he just lost his mind."

"I don't understand. Things seemed so good, and then she cheated on me."

Can you see it? What you choose before marriage is intimately connected to what happens after marriage.

You win at living single, and protect the marriage you'll have one day, when you avoid sexual sin.

6. If You've Not Repented of Sexual Sin, Don't Get Married

If you have not yet abandoned or repented from sexual sin, don't get married.

When people have difficulties in marriage, it's easy to believe the problem is that they chose the wrong person. But, actually, it wasn't necessarily the wrong person; it may have been the wrong *timing*. Wait until God finishes His work in you before you get married.

This is true if you're sleeping with your girlfriend or boyfriend, and it's also true if you have an addiction to pornography. For the sake of your future marriage and for your own sake, avoid porn for all the following reasons:

- Porn objectifies women and men.
- In pornography, emotions don't matter.
- Porn reduces sex to an act.
- Porn tempts people to meet their own needs when God designed us to meet each other's needs.
- Porn rewires our brains and keeps us from being able to experience true intimacy.
- Porn distorts our perceptions of natural human bodies.

Truly, there's no end to the damage that pornography can do to individuals and to couples. If you are tempted by pornography, it's time to handle your business. Get software for your computer to block porn. Identify a wise and faithful friend who can hold you accountable. Embrace fasting as a way to build the spiritual muscle you need to resist temptation.

You win at living single when you postpone marriage—and dating—until you've rejected and repented of your sexual sin.

Maybe you're already married, and you picked this book up off your sister's coffee table. Maybe during your dating or engagement you did fall into sin.

"Pastor, we're married now, so it's all good."

Slow down. It's actually not all good because there's an undertone of unrepented sin in your life—in your marriage. That's going to affect how you interact with your spouse. If you did not care enough about your partner's relationship with God to control yourself before you were married and then stood in front of a pastor and said "I'm going to put you above all else," you may have some work to do together. Maybe you were not Christians before you got married and did not know that sex outside of marriage had spiritual ramifications. Well, now that you know, it's time to surrender your past to Jesus and ask for forgiveness. It's time for a spiritual clean slate.

If you're heading toward the altar and you find yourself in this situation, be sure to discuss it during premarital counseling. Discuss being sexually active before marriage. Deal with the sexual abuse you endured. Be transparent about coming out of an alternative lifestyle. In most marriages, people are bringing a lot from their past, and you want to deal with that before you get married. (And . . . likely afterward as well.)

Back to the singles. I want you to win by avoiding sex outside of marriage, and I know what a challenge that can be. So, take the steps you need to. First, stay connected to God. Be in the Word. Talk to God in prayer. Second, identify friends who will help you date with integrity. Find friends, peers you respect and trust, who you can process with. And find an older mentor who can walk with you. Third, start teaching your body not to respond to every desire it has; fasting decreases the undesired responses of your body and builds spiritual muscle. When you choose to live well, God is going to give you everything you need to succeed.

You win at living single, and you strengthen your eventual relationship with a partner, when you avoid sexual sin.

Now I want to talk about the *pace* of your relationship. I want to encourage you to find a healthy, happy medium between the dangerous "race to the altar" and its equally menacing counterpart, the foot-drag. Let's go . . .

Q: How does a Christian couple recover from having sex before marriage?

A: Let me give you some steps to work through if you find yourself in this situation:

1. Acknowledge it's not God's best, and repent.
2. Enlist accountability from spiritual authority. This needs to be someone who you really don't want to disappoint and who you have given permission to hold you accountable.
3. Set in place healthy boundaries based on your weakest moments, not your strongest ones.
4. Don't keep delaying marriage (#HandleYourBusiness). Get married.

Watch Your Speed

Date at the Right Pace

NOT LONG AFTER HE'D GRADUATED FROM COLLEGE, TONY WAS dating a great girl named Sherree. She loved God, she was in medical school, and she was beautiful. To be honest, he was also beautiful. I'm not sure if men can be beautiful, but he was. Tony was tall, massive, and strong. He was in grad school for engineering. He was a great guy and a solid Christian. His parents' marriage had ended in divorce, and Tony had been deeply affected by it. Tony and Sherree had been dating for four years. Yes, *four*. And after four years, Sherree broke up with Tony. She'd had enough. In fact, she ended up marrying another guy within two years. Today, almost a decade later, she's happily married with three beautiful kids. And Tony? He's still single. Tony was moving too slow.

Damien's story is very different. The word *dating* wasn't even in Damien's vocabulary. In fact, he was only interested in courtship, which is when a couple starts dating with the express intention of marrying. So, when Damien asked Emily's father if he could court her, he already intended their relationship to move toward marriage. Before. Their. First. Date. That, I'm going to suggest, is moving too fast.

Dating with marriage in mind requires avoiding two pitfalls: moving too fast and moving too slow. You want to move at a pace that's just right.

Don't Go Too Fast: Just Say No to Courtship

I hate courtship.

Can we talk about how much I hate the concept of courtship? Under this model of pursuing marriage, there's no taking time to find out if this is even someone you enjoy having conversations with. There's no feeling things out to see if you vibe. There's no pausing to notice if you're attracted to this person. It's like going from zero to a hundred. Courtship implies the promise of a marriage. And if you haven't taken the time to learn about someone, in all the ways, you don't want to make that promise. When you're dating, you're discerning whether or not a relationship might lead to marriage. When you're dating, the only commitment is to not date someone else. The courtship model puts pressure on both parties to marry before they've even gotten to know each other. It leads to frustration and disappointment.

I understand the idea of courtship comes from a desire to intentionally pursue marriage. I think Christians often assume that dating implies casually jumping from person to person, having sex before marriage, or living it up in your young years. That's obviously not what I am endorsing. However, making

implied commitments to marry someone you haven't yet gotten to know is not wise or loving.

The dating I'm referring to does not include living in sin
or going out with someone who you have no intention of
marrying. However, let's be clear: When you're dating someone, you're not required to marry them. (And, for that matter,
when you're engaged to someone, you're not required to marry
them.) When you're *married*? Yeah, then you're all in. But
you'll serve yourself well by slowing down so that you don't
rush into marriage with someone who might not be the best
fit for you for any number of reasons.

It's not just the idea of courtship that gets on my nerves.
When I see couples who've just met each other praying together regularly, I tell them they need to *slow down*. It's too
much too soon. Prayer is intimate. And why would I bring you
into an intimate space when you may not be around three
months from now? So, I don't think it's wise to pray together
on a regular basis when you're dating. Similarly, in the first
months of a relationship, you don't need to be fasting together
to determine if you should take your commitment to the next
level. Settle down.

Do I think that prayer and fasting are weird and bad? No.
Just do it by yourself, in silence.

I admit, it's a gray area. Couples who are engaged might
find it really useful to pray together. I'm not trying to offer
hard-and-fast rules. But be cautious about going deep together,
spiritually, too fast.

You might be saying, "Wow, this is a lot. Don't go too fast,
but be intentional and date with a purpose. Do I go forward?
Do I slow down? Which is it?" The key is balance. Yes, move
forward and be intentional—just not at a speed that can become impossible to control.

You remember the movies you had to watch in driver's ed? There was that crash test dummy that would get crumpled up into the steering wheel or thrown out of the vehicle when the driver exceeded the speed limit. Don't be a crash dummy.

Don't drive too fast.

Don't Go Too Slow: Don't Date for Five Years

Here's my personal opinion: Don't date for more than two years. It doesn't take a grown adult that long to make a decision. Now, when I've said that before and it's been posted online, people have had plenty to say.

I dated my husband for thirteen years, and we're good.

We dated for five years, and now we've been married for forty-seven years.

I had to wait six years until that man proposed. But I got him.

Everyone loves it when their story is the exception to the rule. But—as a rule—you don't want to be dating for years and years. It likely won't end well for you.

Brothers, handle your business. Fish or cut bait. If you've dated for two years, either put a ring on it or call it quits. It doesn't have to be two years on the dot, but you get the idea.

Sisters, you don't have to wait around forever. You can cut bait too!

You might be thinking, *What if I'm in high school or a freshman in college? Is two years realistic for me?* Brace yourself. My answer: I said what I said. I'm not saying you need to legalistically stick to 730 days and not one day past. I am saying if marriage is not in the near future, don't start on the journey. In other words, if you don't see yourself getting married anytime soon, my best advice is to not date and instead focus on spiritual growth. If you will be intentional in your pursuit of Christ during high school and your early college years, you'll be much better prepared to date with integrity, character, and Christ-likeness when the time comes.

There are lots of reasons why moving too slowly when you're dating can be harmful to you and your relationship.

One of the reasons that dating for years on end can be harmful is that you may begin *playing* at marriage. When you date someone for many years—and especially if you're sleeping together—you are pretending like you're married. You're making life plans and decisions with someone who hasn't committed to you.

I see women postponing grad school because it's inconvenient for a boyfriend who's never committed—and then he leaves! That woman who waited around for five years, until he left, could have been three years into her career, but she was waiting on a man who was never going to commit.

Dating Puts You in a Holding Pattern in Life

If you're on a flight and there's a storm as your airplane approaches its destination, the air traffic controllers will likely instruct the pilot to *wait* to land. The plane maintains a holding pattern. Dating can be a little bit like a holding pattern. Let's say you're dating, and you have it in your heart to purchase a home.

If we get married, we might be able to buy a bigger house.
If we get married, we may not want to live in this part of town.
I'll just hold off on buying the house to see where this goes.

Maybe you wait five years for someone who isn't going to commit, and once the relationship ends, you realize that you were holding off for . . . nothing.

Would it be ideal for you to have all your ducks in a row before becoming engaged? Sure. In a perfect world, you'd have finished your education, launched your career, climbed out of debt, and bought a home. Maybe it's ideal, but is it realistic? Not at all.

Someone asked me if there's a checklist of things to have in order before getting married. And while it might be comforting to have that list and be able to check off the boxes, a person's maturity is actually more important. And maturity is evidenced in a life plan.

> Does the person you want to marry see themselves finishing their education?
> Do they see the moves they'd like to make in a career?
> Do they imagine a future that includes building a family?

What's more important than checking all those boxes is actually being a mature person who has a vision for life.

Do Move Forward When There's Vision and a Plan

Let's pause and talk about submission for a minute. That may have felt like a quick pivot, but I heard a great preacher break down the word *submission* as "sub + mission."

And he went further to say that submission, when it comes to a wife supporting her husband, means "supporting the mission." When the Bible says, "Submit yourselves to your own husbands," it is inviting wives to come alongside their husbands to support the vision for their families.[1]

Now, if that man ain't got no vision, there's nothing for you to submit to. Nothing for you to support. I hear plenty of women balking, resisting: "I don't like this idea of submitting to my husband." And this is why I'm challenging you right now, sister, as you're considering *who* you date and *how* you date, to be looking for someone to whose mission you believe in and could support.

Does he have a financial plan?
Does he have plans to build a family?
Does he have a plan to pay for children's education?
Does he have a plan for how to live out his faith in his
    family?
Does he have a plan for his career?
Does he have a plan for retirement?
Does he have a plan for how to care for older parents?

If homey got no plan, you don't want him.

When I mention wives submitting to their husbands, I'm not talking about a woman being a victim of this idiot without a plan whom she's got to follow everywhere. Before you marry him, ask him what his plan is. You decide whether it's a mission you want to support.

Sometimes, a young man—as young as sixteen—will have a plan. He knows that he's going to graduate high school, enlist in the army, do three years of service, go to college for free, and finally become an officer. He's got a plan. But that's *rare*, right? I won't lie. I was that young weirdo with a plan at sixteen. I knew I was going to college to get my degree and then I was going to be in full-time ministry while pursuing business ventures on the side. Two decades later, that's exactly what I'm doing. And, to be fair, there's likely a good reason for that. My mom was diagnosed with cancer when I was thirteen. My sister had three brain surgeries. I had to grow up faster than most sixteen-year-olds.

But what we're seeing today is that young adults are delaying ownership of adult responsibilities. Like that twenty-five-year-old who's living in his parents' basement playing video games. Or the thirtysomething who's not at all concerned about getting married or starting a family. Years ago, boomers accused millennials of being entitled, but now we millennials are accusing Gen Zers of just being thrill seekers. They don't really want to work. At seventeen, they want to travel to Dubai and vacation in the Maldives. Maybe they were raised by Gen Xers who worked themselves to the bone, and they don't want that.

Although the people of one generation are never all one way, you do want to run from the people who are avoiding responsibilities. That's not what you're looking for. You're looking for someone with a plan, someone with vision.

Date at the Right Pace

When you're on this journey toward marriage, you want to date at the right pace. If you're moving too quickly, you could be marrying someone you don't even know. (And might not care to know, which you would have realized if you'd slowed it down and taken your time.) If you're moving too slowly, you could be jeopardizing the kind of thriving relationship you want to have eventually with the person to whom you'll be married. If you insist on getting every single last daggum duck in a row before you pull the trigger, you're never going to be ready. You'll be stuck in a holding pattern.

When you have a vision, make a plan. Execute the plan. Boom.

As you're traveling with your boo at a healthy pace, I'm encouraging you to keep your eyes open for warning signs: yellow flags and red flags. Keep reading to learn what you don't want to miss . . .

Rom-Coms That Give Us Hope

1. *Nobody's Fool*
Takeaway: The one who seems the least likely might be the best one.

2. *Always Be My Maybe*
Takeaway: Even when it takes a few decades, love will find a way.

3. *How to Lose a Guy in 10 Days*
Takeaway: Love can find people who don't even want a relationship.

4. *Just Wright*
Takeaway: Love can take us by surprise.

5. *Last Holiday*
Takeaway: Love goes to the ends of the earth.

Heed the Warning Signs

Don't Ignore the Cautionary Flags

LET ME SHARE A STORY OF THREE FIRST DATES.

Jorge and Wendy met on a dating app. They messaged back and forth for almost six weeks and got to the point where they felt comfortable and were super excited to meet in person. Wendy was discovering that Jorge was a serious Christian. He had a great job and was a leader at his church. Their first date at a local pizzeria was a dream. They had great chemistry. They talked for two hours, even after the bill had been paid and dinner was clearly over. (Oh yes, he definitely paid the bill.) And they found that they had common goals, common values, common dreams. Before they ended the first date, they were already planning the second. It was all green flags for Jorge and Wendy.

Elise and Kamari met at church. On their first date, brunch at Waffle House, they shared their stories with each other. Elise had always wanted to do hair and was working at a salon she was in the process of purchasing. Kamari had wanted to be a teacher and work with kids, but when he was in undergrad, his mother insisted that he do something else. She persuaded him to study medicine, and so he went to medical school and became a urologist. As Elise listened, she saw Kamari's mood change; she could tell he wasn't happy with the path he was on. She was curious, though she didn't press the issue since it was just a first date. But it was a yellow flag for Elise.

Keith and Angelica met at the grocery store. (Yes, it can happen.) On their first date, as they played mini golf, the two talked about their lives and had a great time. After golf, they stopped by a casual dining restaurant. While Keith ordered a Coke, Angelica started with a glass of wine. Then another. Then she ordered a cocktail. Then she ordered a beer. By the time she invited Keith back to her place "for a drink," Keith had lost interest. Angelica's drinking was a red flag.

When you date, you're getting to know someone. You're noticing the green flags and the yellow ones and the red ones. And if you haven't compromised your values, and you still feel like they're not the person for you, you can part ways having had a good experience—or at least an interesting one.

Pay attention.

I will say that one red flag does not have to be a dealbreaker; the person you're getting to know might be having a really bad day. But it does mean that you are on high alert. You're paying attention. You're not rationalizing away troubling behavior.

Green Flags

If you're seeing green flags, that's awesome. Congrats.

But we do know that sometimes when we're in lust—I mean "love"!—our vision can get a little wonky. We can have some issues with color blindness. So if you *think* you're seeing all green, I'm going to need you to run that by your community. Get the person you are dating around your family, friends, and spiritual mentors. Let those who love you confirm the green flags you are seeing.

Yellow Flags

I want you to have your eyes open for the yellow flags.

In car racing, a yellow flag signals that there's been a crash, there's debris on the track, or there's some other kind of similar issue. And that flag is going to be waving at the beginning of the problematic zone. When you see that flag, you know to be cautious. And everyone's got to hold their positions too. There's no passing when you see the yellow flag. It's similar to the yellow traffic lights you heed on the street. If you're driving correctly, a yellow light means that you're going to slow down, not speed up.

I want to throw out some yellow flags you might see when you're dating. To be clear, these are different than red ones. Red means you should stop immediately and assess if it is safe to proceed or if the journey should be abandoned.

When you're dating, there's no reason to be in a rush. So when you encounter one of these yellow flags, just slow down; acknowledge and address it.

Race and Culture

You may still be single if you've told God what race your spouse has to be.

What's that now, Pastor?

You may have cut off who God has for you because you've predetermined that they can only come in one skin color. (Mic drop.)

Yeah, I just went there.

This said, I want to acknowledge that dating someone of a different race, ethnicity, or culture can bring its own unique challenges. For instance, different cultures may have different definitions of the roles of men and women. And different values related to work. And money. And everything. If you marry cross-culturally, you'll face complexities in your marriage. (The real: You'll also face complexities when you come from the same race or culture.)

And when you date or marry someone from another race, ethnicity, or culture, you have to acknowledge that there's more to consider than just the two of you. There are your families. And while the attitudes of your families and friends don't have to be deal-breakers, they're definitely worth considering. If the attitudes toward race that your family and friends embrace are going to make life uncomfortable for the person you're dating, or the one you hope to marry, then handling their foolishness is on you. Don't expect your partner to muster up all of the energy and fortitude to constantly educate or correct your people. Don't expect them to armor up, emotionally, to survive Thanksgiving dinner with Uncle Joe.

If God brings you a partner of a different race, take all the time you need to make sure you're facing the differences together—both inside your relationship and outside of it.

At our church, about half of our members are African American, and 40 percent more are African. They live here in the United States now, but they started their lives in Africa—or their parents did. And because I've performed weddings and done premarital counseling for Africans marrying African Americans, I can assure you that having a similar hue of skin does not protect you from the differences you'll face when you marry someone who doesn't share your cultural experience. Specifically, I've known African parents who refuse to give their blessing to a child marrying an African American.

But let's go even further. There are Africans who don't want their children marrying someone who comes from their same country but a different tribe.

It's prejudiced.

It's racist.

And when a man or a woman is in love, they'll often ignore their parents' wishes (especially in America!), and in many cases they should.

Not having the support of in-laws or future in-laws is not a deal-breaker, but you've got to be really sober about facing that reality. I tell folks, "If your parents don't approve of your spouse because of their race or some cultural difference, I'm not saying, 'Don't marry them.' I'm saying, 'Slow down, and at least try to change your parents' minds.'" You may never change their minds, but you won't regret slowing down and trying to win them over. As frustrating as their ignorance is, their support can be tremendously helpful and really does matter.

When you have your first kids, it's a gift to have in-laws who are there to hold the baby while you sleep. When you don't have that, it makes those early weeks and months a lot harder. And if your family is behind the marriage, they're going to come alongside you both.

If God brings you a partner who was raised in a different culture, recognize that as a yellow flag and invest in discovering how to best navigate it together.

Bringing Children into a Marriage

Let's imagine another kind of scenario.

Sister, let's say that you have saved yourself for marriage. And let's say that the man to whom you are engaged has two children from two different women.

That's gonna be hard. You will have to navigate relationships with two other women. You will likely have insecurities around his relationship with his children or your relationship with his children as things get more serious. You are also likely going to be wondering why things did not work out with your man and the other two women.

You two are in different seasons of life. You've had different experiences. Don't minimize it. There's a reason your family is concerned.

I'm not telling you that you should write him off because he has kids and you waited for marriage. But I am saying there's a good chance y'all are not as compatible as you think. Which means you're going to face challenges and difficulties that you wouldn't have to face otherwise. Don't be so prideful that you think you're the exception to the rule.

Bringing kids into a marriage isn't a deal-breaker. But it is a yellow flag—something you should give careful thought to. Proceed with caution. Slow down. Bring in godly counselors who will ask you important questions. Pray for wisdom. Release your pride.

Red Flags

All right, we were just getting warmed up with those yellow flags. It's about to get real now: *red* flags.

The Way They Express, or Don't Express, Their Emotions

One of the biggest red flags you might notice in a relationship is when the person you're dating exhibits an unhealthy emotional response to the natural events they face in life.

Now, I'm going to guess that your mind may have gone to the scenario where he gets a crack in his windshield and explodes in a fiery rage. Or her sister borrowed her mascara without asking and she blew a gasket. And I'll agree that those are red flags to watch out for. You know this.

But I'm encouraging you to notice when someone's emotional response to an event is less than you might expect.

She gets a huge promotion at work, and she's not interested in celebrating it.

He gets a perfect score on his MCAT, and he kind of blows it off.

Celebration, rejoicing, and elation are normal, healthy responses when we experience goodness in our lives. If that kind of natural response is absent in the person you're dating, you might be dealing with someone who doesn't know how to show emotion.

And I'm going to caution you further by noting that we can often *reward* this kind of emotional response. If someone achieves a monumental accomplishment and brushes it off, we might even spiritualize it by calling them "humble." Be careful. If you grew up with explosions of emotion in your home, it might feel comforting to be with someone who stays even-keeled emotionally. But fifteen years into marriage, when you finally accept that this person can't feel much of anything, it's not going to feel comforting. It's going to feel really lonely.

A guy I'll call James was dating a woman who seemed to have it all together. She was successful in Hollywood and thriving professionally. But one evening, James was out with his friends and had forgotten to take his phone with him. So, he missed her calls over a period of about three hours. And the woman James was dating completely *lost* it. I mean . . . major meltdown. Like James had never seen before.

"You don't love me. You don't care about me. You don't value me!"

She didn't respond in a natural, healthy way to a few missed phone calls.

Hear me: We're *going* to have feelings when things go wrong. Of course. If a guy is supposed to pick you up for a date and he's twenty minutes late, it's natural to feel frustrated. But furious for the whole evening? Giving him the silent treatment? Raging for the next three days?

Both extreme emotion and a lack of emotion are red flags you need to acknowledge.

Shadiness

If the person you're interested in doesn't want to be around community? Red flag. Women, I want you to be very leery of a guy who doesn't want to spend time with your family or your friends. Guys, same deal.

I encourage those who are dating to do activities with groups of people—friends from work or church, and especially your family and mentors. Some people don't want to hang out in groups because they're shady and don't have good intentions. If you're with somebody who says, "Hey, let's just not be too public with this thing. Let's not have titles or labels. Let's just talk on the phone all night long. Let's just DM. Let's meet up at random places, at random times. Let's see where it goes."

Nope.

You don't want to wait and see where it goes because it's *dark*. You can't see anything. Y'all need to turn some lights on. Put a spotlight on this thing so you can see. I'm not saying you have to give hourly updates about your relationship on social media or make things Facebook official after a few dates; that's not healthy either. But when no one in your community has met the person you're dating or even knows that you're dating (and your partner wants it that way), that's a red flag.

God ain't shady. I know this for sure because Scripture assures us,

> God is light; in him there is no darkness at all. If we claim to have fellowship with him and yet walk in the darkness, we lie and do not live out the truth. But if we walk in the light, as he is in the light, we have fellowship with one another, and the blood of Jesus, his Son, purifies us from all sin.[1]

You Know the Other Red Flags: Pay Attention

Red flags should be fairly obvious. You know them: substance abuse, violence, infidelity, and others.

But let's talk about how you handle those red flags. For instance, maybe you wanted to believe they were *yellow* flags. Maybe you've tried to ignore them, or justify them, for whatever reason. Maybe you tolerated his outbursts and his violence toward others because his rage hadn't yet been directed at you. I do understand how tempting it can be to rationalize this behavior when other parts of the relationship are satisfying.

If you're dating someone now and recognize poor behavior, or if you tolerated it in the past, I encourage you to look in the mirror and ask: "What's the heart issue I'm dealing with? Why would I tolerate this in my life?"

This is actually a great exercise you can do with God as you review your past relationships. What did you put up with for too long? Offer that to God with a humble heart, and seek His insight. This is one of the ways you get healthy *before* entering your next relationship.

Don't Shut Your Eyes

Have you ever driven in the mountains? If so, you might have seen some yellow warning signs letting you know about sharp upcoming turns or winding roads. And you know what happens if you ignore one of those signs? Or if you're peeking at your phone and miss it? You. Drive. Off. The. Road. You crash and die.

I understand how tempting it can be to ignore the yellow and red flags we're seeing. If a yellow flag is causing concern, we may fool ourselves into believing that it will change with time. Or we may want to wait and get more intel. Or when we see a red flag, we may rationalize and say, "It's not *that* bad." It's not as bad as what someone else has in their relationship. Bottom line? We don't always see clearly. And that's why we need to date with the support of our communities. Let them have your back. Keep reading.

The following practices might distract you from thinking care-fully about dating. Here are some hazards to watch out for as you seek to date with integrity.

 What is glazing? Glazing is when you incessantly compliment someone to the point that it's annoying.

 What is cuffing season? Cuffing is when you are in an exclusive relationship. And "cuffing season"—in the winter months, often considered the period between Thanksgiving and Valentine's Day—is when singles may feel lonely, as they're trapped inside, and look to get together with someone.

 What is benching? This term describes the act of keeping someone on the sidelines while you explore other options. It's like having a "bench" of potential partners but never quite committing to any of them. This behavior can leave the person feeling confused and uncertain about where they stand in the relationship.

 What is breadcrumbing? When someone shows you just enough interest to keep you intrigued but never enough to truly commit to a relationship, it's known as breadcrumbing. They'll send occasional messages or likes on social media, but when it comes to making plans or having meaningful conversations, they're always elusive.[2]

 What is the ick factor? The ick factor is a sudden feeling of repulsion toward someone you're dating. This disgust seems to come out of nowhere. It may be precipitated by the partner saying or doing something cringeworthy, but it also might not be connected to any antecedent.

Travel with Others

Do Not Date in Isolation

ANDREA, A TWENTY-EIGHT-YEAR-OLD WORKING AS A CAMPUS minister in Southern California, had asked God to lead her to the man she would marry. She was the woman every man should be looking for: She was intelligent; she loved God; she was a high-capacity leader; she was attractive and kind. Andrea started spending time with a guy named Chad. Chad identified as a Christian, and he had grown up in church. Maybe he didn't *love* God, but he *liked* God.

Sensing that the relationship was moving forward, she scheduled coffee with Jamesa, a spiritually mature friend she trusted. Jamesa had been married for seven years. Andrea shared who Chad was and how they'd been hanging out and getting to know each other. She kind of brain dumped every-thing she knew about him.

Andrea summed it up: "I'm really interested in this guy, and we're thinking about dating. What do you think?"

To be clear, Andrea had done everything right by inviting a trustworthy friend into this process.

Before answering, Jamesa considered all that Andrea had shared and paused to gather her words.

"I'm concerned," she began. "I'm concerned that he is not mature enough to lead you. His faith doesn't seem to be a pri-ority. And I see that he has a job but not a career. No aspira-tions. From what you shared with me, he doesn't have a vision for his life."

Andrea's face fell.

Jamesa continued, "He's never taken on major responsi-bilities in life, and he's not managing the ones he has with maturity."

Andrea looked away but kept listening.

"You, on the other hand," her friend said, "are a leader among leaders. You have a vision for your life, and you know where you're going."

Then she gently shared with Andrea that she'd seen a lot of girls marry men because they wanted to be married. But when the woman was far more mature and responsible than the guy, a few years into the marriage her eyes would be opened. She'd begin to feel like his mom. Like she had to carry him through the hard seasons.

Boldly, Jamesa counseled, "I don't want that for you. I don't think you should date this guy."

As Andrea wiped away a tear, her friend's heart broke for her.

As you know, after this conversation, Andrea had a decision to make. And she ended up breaking things off with Chad. For the next six months she fell into depression. She avoided her friend.

And about a year and a half later, Andrea ended up meeting the man of her dreams. They were married one year after they met, and today she is as happy as can be and grateful to her honest friend!

Submit to Godly Counsel: Who, When, Where

In a book of biblical wisdom, the writer of Proverbs announced, "By wise counsel thou shalt make thy war: and in multitude of counsellors there is safety" (24:6, KJV). You need people in your life whom you trust. You need to let trusted friends get to know the person you choose to date. You need people who are not all tied up in the situation who can tell you what is up.

Let's dish about submission again. (And it's not just for women.) Not only do you need to be submitted to God, but you also need to be submitted to the people in your life whose values and discernment you trust. You need to ask, "What do you think?" And you need to submit to their response.

No, actually, let me get a little more specific. Because when we're talking about submitting or listening to counsel, you do not always have to go with the "yes" of your adviser. Have you ever had a parent try to hook you up with somebody? You're just like, "Seriously?" No, you don't have to go with their "yes." But I caution you: Please hardly ever go against their "no." You need people around you that you trust.

Can I just help you out? You need all kinds of people to walk this journey with you. You need ones who are older than you—we'll get into that in the next chapter. You need people who are married. You need ones who are single. Now, I do want you to include those who know you best, but I'll admit that your friends don't always help. Sometimes they're just as dumb as you are. And chances are, they want to date your boyfriend if you break up with him, so they're a little compromised. You need wise, godly counselors—across all ages—who can tell you, "Yes, that's it," or "No, that's not it." And you need them to tell you why. You need people around you who are invested in helping you learn and grow.

There are three things you need counsel in.

1. You Need Wise Counsel About the "Who"

You need counsel in *who* to date. I love God. And even as a younger man, I was fully confident in my ability to hear God. Except when it came to a wife. I knew before I even went down that road that when it came to discerning who she would be, I couldn't necessarily trust what I was hearing. Because I knew that whatever I heard could have been just me speaking. It could have been God speaking. Or it could have been the devil speaking. And I would not know the difference. So, I chose to submit to those I trust.

When Zai and I were dating, Pastor Wayne, one of my mentors, and his wife, CeCe, visited us in Maryland and met Zai for the first time. We were sitting at dinner when Pastor Wayne said to her, "Wow, I know so much about you." She looked at me, and then she looked at him like, *Wait, what in the world?*

And before I could even open my mouth, Pastor Wayne said, "Oh yeah, Pastor Stephen has been telling me about you."

This man did not stop.

"Yeah," he continued. "Like for months and months and months. I remember when you did this . . . and you went here . . . and when you did that. . . ."

And I was just like, "Pastor Wayne, come on, man. Stop."

You know what that's called? It's called *wisdom*. Because I know that I'm not smart enough to get this homeboy to the promised land by myself.

2. You Need Wise Counsel About the "When"

The second thing you need to seek counsel about is *when*.

Zai had been at my church for two years and was a top leader before we started dating. I had told myself I would never date any woman in the church because if I were to date and break up with someone in the congregation, it could undermine people's respect for me as their senior pastor. I didn't consider anyone in the church until my mother came to me and said my rule was stupid if it kept me from dating a great woman like Zai. I don't know if I then got too eager, but soon after that my mom changed her tune and asked me to let her pray about Zai before I made a move. This woman of God prayed for three months straight, with me checking in at minimum weekly—but more often daily. What did I do? I waited for my mom's blessing; I did this not because she is my mom but because she is one of my spiritual mentors and I respect and value her counsel. My mom later revealed that she felt if Zai and I went on one date, we'd get married. As a result, she was praying for confirmation on a wife, not a girlfriend.

Once I got that go-ahead, I asked Zai out on a Tuesday. That Friday, we went on our first date. Two and a half months later, we were engaged. What am I saying? Submit your timing to *counsel*. I admit that our pace was on the . . . rapid side . . . but we knew each other for a long time before we ever started dating. I also know that, especially today, many have the tendency to wait way too long.

3. You Need Wise Counsel About the "Where"

Finally, submit your counsel to *where.*

When I was in college, my grandmother lived in a new development in New Jersey. And her street hadn't yet been added to my outdated Garmin GPS. So, whenever I'd drive up to visit her, I'd call my dad for a reminder of what road I had to turn on to reach her neighborhood. I couldn't have made it where I was going without my dad's guidance. And I'm going to suggest that you're not going to make it through this dating journey unscathed if you don't invite others to help you navigate where your relationship happens.

When I say "where," I'm talking about *boundaries.* (Just couldn't think of a *w* word for it.) Exercise smart boundaries, and allow your adviser to check in on whether you are keeping those boundaries. Don't make them hunt you down. Don't make them ask you a million questions. And, obviously, counsel is only helpful if you tell the truth. But you need somebody else involved.

One of our staff values at the church is that we are not that holy. (Not a typo.) We understand that we are human and susceptible to falling. So, we value transparency. There's safety when you're not running by yourself. Here is one simple, wise boundary that will help you make good decisions as you date: Don't ever be alone with the person you are dating in a house, dorm room, or apartment. No. If you don't create that boundary, you are setting yourself up to be a casualty. And listen to me: If you've already blown it, if you've already messed up, I do not condemn you. There is grace. God can restore you and get you back on your journey of purity. But there is no reason to go through that pain if you do not have to.

And you don't.

Let your trusted advisers speak into the "who," the "when," and the "where" (#boundaries).

When You're Dating, You Need Peers Beside You

Don't date in isolation.

You need to build friendships with peers who are the same sex as you. And this isn't just about dating; it's about walking your journey with Christ well. Only a man can teach a man to be a man. Only a woman can teach a woman to be a woman. You need to nurture friendships with friends who follow Jesus for the sake of becoming who God made you to be.

But there's another reason. *If you can't maintain healthy friendships, you probably won't be able to maintain a healthy marriage.* That's because friendships are like the entry level when it comes to serving someone else and not getting anything out of it.

> Friendship is where you learn to believe in someone else's dreams.
> Friendship is where you show up, even when it doesn't benefit you.
> Friendship is where you cheer someone else on as they run their race.
> Friendship is where you celebrate somebody else.

If you're not doing that in friendships, it's going to be very difficult to do it in marriage.

Ideally, you had siblings and so this type of friendship started in childhood. If you weren't able to celebrate your siblings, it's going to be hard to celebrate a friend. And it's going to be hard to celebrate a spouse.

I think we see the beauty of a godly friendship in the lives of David and Jonathan.[1] We can look at the posture with which they loved each other. And this is the posture we're after in our own friendships. Here are some attitudes I would encourage you to adopt toward your close friends:

> I'm going to do everything I can do to help the call of
>   God on your life come to pass.
> I'm committed to you.
> In my commitment to you, I'm going to point out some
>   blind spots.

Will there be tough times when we dare to have hard conversations with friends? Yes. The writer of Proverbs advised, "Faithful are the wounds of a friend" (27:6, KJV). That means that the wounds of a friend can be *trusted*.

Do you have anyone in your life today who loves you enough to wound you?

Are you healthy enough to invite the wounds of a friend without retaliating?

Let's say two college friends are each dating a different woman. These two guys have given each other permission to point out blind spots. They have permission to get up in each other's business. That's the win, right there.

I had guys in college who cared for me by speaking the truth.

They pressed, "Dude, you need to ask her out. Stop being a punk."

They pushed, "You know enough about her. Stop dancing around it."

Or they prodded, "You know she came stumbling out of that frat party. Three weeks in a row. That's not wifey material."

Now, I wanted that kind of input from my friends, but I

know we've also seen it go the other way. We all know that friend who got mad because they didn't want to hear the truth. So they torpedoed a friendship and kept the dating relationship. Until they didn't. Then—like in any good Hallmark movie—they came back with their tail between their legs.

"I should have listened to you."

When you invite your community to offer godly counsel, submit to it. Especially when they're encouraging you to slow down or cut things off with the person you are dating. Welcome counsel from those who love you and want the best for you. Don't be quick to dismiss it.

Date Around Others

Date around friends and family. In other words, keep friends and family near as you pursue a relationship with someone of the opposite sex.

Now, I know that today a lot of people's families are broken down or distant. They live across the country. They may be absent from your life. They may even be apathetic. And you may have grown accustomed to being on your own. But I'm also convinced that God wants us to be living life, and dating, in community. And, in part, that's the church's job. That's what it means that God "sets the lonely in families."[2] It's the church's job to create safe places for people to meet. It's the church's job to care for you when she breaks your heart. It's the church's job to celebrate with you when he finally puts a ring on it. Let the church be the church in your life by allowing them to share your journey.

And let them join your dates. ("Wait, what's that now, Pastor? 'Cause there ain't enough room in my pickup truck . . .") Okay, how about you let them join your pre-dates (i.e., the hangouts that aren't official dates)? Listen up: You don't need to have lots of private one-on-one time early in your relationship when you barely know the person. One of the best ways to get to know someone is in a group. You're still going to have the opportunity to discover what you need to know about this person, but you've also got the added benefits of others' insights, accountability, and more. Go out with groups of friends.

Too often people start dating and then cut off everybody from their life. It becomes this Bonnie-and-Clyde situation. (Y'all, Bonnie and Clyde *died*. They did not make it to the end of the movie. Isolation didn't work out for them.) Don't isolate yourselves.

If you don't want to fall in love with an axe murderer, it's gonna take a friend, a sibling, an auntie, or a mother and a father—either the parents who raised you or your spiritual parents—to say, "I know you love them, but they are crazy." You need the safety that you get in community.

Who You Want in Your Corner

You want people in your community to help you vet the person you're dating. And when I say "vet," I mean that this adviser is specifically helping you consider whether this is a person you could marry. But you don't need the opinion of every joker in your orbit. The homey or the girlfriend in the next cubicle at work who has a radically different lifestyle than you isn't the person whose counsel you need to seek.

Something I've seen in the church is this catty business where a friend will say, "He's not the one for you" or "She's not the one" because that friend is *jealous*. They want the kind of relationship you have. Or maybe two girls like the same guy. And once one of those girls starts dating him, the other one has nothing good to say about him. (Sis, you're mad because he wasn't interested in *you*.) Don't be quick to dismiss pushback, but it is important to recognize that not all pushback is valid or helpful. And definitely have older adults speaking into your dating life.

Know who to invite in. *When looking for someone to help vet the person you are dating, look for someone who shares your values and goals.* This is vital because there are going to be important people in your life, possibly even your parents, who aren't Christians, who don't share your values. Now, if you have a healthy relationship with a parent who follows Christ, they *absolutely* need to be involved before you get engaged. And there's actually something to be gained from the honest assessment of parents who don't walk with God.

There's not a big laundry list of criteria for the person you want to help you discern whether someone would make a good partner for you. Simply look for someone who shares your values and goals.

And I'll say that because your family knows what makes you tick, you want them to weigh in. Ideally, that includes your parents. I also know that not all parents can be trusted. So, if your racist parents are the only people who are like, "This is not from God," but your pastor and another person of God say they have peace about it, you can weigh those opinions and give some more weight than others.

This said, if your family's not on board, slow down and do the work to make it happen. Maybe you sit down and say, "Hey, this is going to happen with or without your blessing. So y'all might as well give your blessing and get involved." Do that work to get your family involved because it matters.

When Sam and Ronetta were dating, and then engaged, both sets of parents were very involved. Five years later, when this couple announced that they wanted to divorce, both sets of parents showed up.

"We'll take the kids for the weekend, and y'all gonna find a marriage counselor and figure this out because we don't do divorce in this family."

And they came in and took the kids, and now decades later, Sam and Ronetta are still married. They didn't just make it work; they cultivated a thriving marriage thanks to the counsel, concern, and involvement of supportive, godly family members stepping up.

Don't date in isolation.

And I specifically want to encourage you to seek out older mentors. These are the travelers who've been on the road for a minute; they have learned a thing or two. I promise you that they are *dropping wisdom*. Keep reading to discover more about finding and utilizing these guides.

More Pickup Lines (Use at Your Own Risk)

"Hey, girl. I thought happiness started with *H,* but why does mine start with *U*?"

"Now I know why Solomon had seven hundred wives . . . because he never met you."

"Better late than never but never late is better."[3]

"I didn't believe in predestination before tonight."

"Do I know you? No? You must just be the girl of my dreams."

Rely on Seasoned Travelers

Seek the Wisdom of Older Mentors

AS I MENTIONED EARLIER, ZAI HAD BEEN A PART OF THE CHURCH for two years before we started dating. We were around each other several times a week among friends, in small groups, at conferences, and in all these other situations. (And, by the way, she was twisted the whole time. If she says otherwise, she lyin'.) One of the reasons we didn't date for those first two years is because I had made an inner vow that I was not going to date any women in the church. I was young and single. I figured if I dated a girl in the church, and then we broke up, that would be a "church split." There would be problems.

I went to every other church in the DMV area where I lived—every young adults group, every worship night, every prayer gathering. I was up there with one hand lifted, one eye open, asking, *Is it her, Lord? Is that her? Or is that her?*

I still remember the first time I saw Zai walk into church. She was gorgeous. I can tell you today what she was wearing.

Well, as she was getting involved at the church, Zai developed a friendship with my mother. I liked her the whole time, but I was trying my best to ignore her because of my rule.

One day my mom comes to me and says, "Bruh . . ." (Yes, my mom really talked like that.)

She said, "If you don't ask that girl out, you are crazy."

Boom.

It's September, and I tell my mom, "I'm going to ask her out."

But my mom says, "No, no, no. Don't ask her out yet. Let me pray about it."

"Mom," I protested, "you just said to ask her out."

"I know. I know," she answered. "But just let me pray about it."

Go on ahead, Mom.

She prays. She prays for the entire month of September. October passes, and there's still no answer from my mom.

She's like, "I'm still praying."

Ugh.

Around that time, after evening worship, Zai and I were chatting in the parking lot. And she was kind of ranting about something hypothetical, but then it suddenly felt like it was no longer hypothetical.

"You know," she said, "Christian men are just pansies."

Yeah, that happened.

"They don't know what they want. They see a good woman, and they don't know how to ask her out. And that's why I'm just over it. They have their time, and if they don't move, I'm moving on."

There are only two people in this conversation, and she's clearly talking to me.

In my head, I'm screaming, *Look, woman! I would ask you out if I could, but I'm waiting for permission.*

I know at this point you are probably thinking, *Major mama's boy.* And you wouldn't be wrong. However, in my defense, my parents weren't just my parents; they were my pastors. I had made a decision a long time prior to submit my life to spiritual authority and allow God to guide me through the people He placed over me.

November goes by, and my mom hasn't decided.

"Mom, are you finished praying?"

In case she didn't understand the urgency, I had to make it plain: "Mom, you're married. You're having sex. This isn't fair."

That's when she understood how serious I was. I know marriage is more than just sex, but your boy was burning.

The first Sunday in December—but really, who's keeping track?—my mom weighs in.

"Okay," she announces, "I prayed about it. She's sticking around long enough that I have a peace about it."

My mom later told me, "I knew you. And I knew Zai. And if you guys went out on one date, you were gonna get married. So I just wanted to make sure it was the right person."

My mom said she had a peace about me dating Zai on a Sunday. Tuesday I asked Zai out after worship night. And you know how that turned out.

Dating was never meant to be just two individuals trying to figure things out. Looking back now, after more than a decade of marriage, I am so glad I submitted and waited. I lost nothing by waiting those three months and gained a level of peace that words can't describe. Zai and I often refer back to that season and talk about how knowing that we didn't begin our journey toward marriage in isolation anchored us and helped alleviate the "Did I marry the right person?" thoughts that every couple faces at one point or another.

When You're Dating, You Need Mentors Above You: Direct Mentoring

I tried to navigate dating with wisdom, and I know you are seeking to do the same. We need older, wiser guides in our lives to help us.

Back in the day, when you got lost while driving, there wasn't GPS to help you get back on track. (Yes, it's true.) So you had to stop at the nearest gas station to ask for directions. If you were lucky, you'd land at one of those local stations where there was a tow truck driver who knew the local roads like the back of his hand. That's the guy you wanted to get guidance from.

When you're dating, you need older spiritual mentors who have your back. Maybe, like me, you have a godly, praying parent. Or it might be your pastor or other older, wiser individuals at your church. There's such a thing as having "holy jealousy" for the life of someone older than you—because you're seeing a life that's submitted to God, and that's what you want. That's who you want on your team.

When I was twenty years old, I had the opportunity to drive to a conference with a mentor, an older pastor. He was probably in his mid-fifties. We had three hours in the car together on our way to this conference in Virginia. Well, I was taking *notes.*

During the course of that drive, Pastor Carlos called his wife twice.

Okay, I'm watching.

Halfway there, he stops at a department store, explaining, "Hey, I gotta run into Macy's and grab my wife a gift."

I see you.

That evening, the conference put the two of us up in a hotel together. Two queen beds. And at about ten o'clock, I hear this guy having a lil' *pillow talk* with his wife! Now, it wasn't anything you couldn't say in front of another person, but it was sweet. I heard him saying to the woman to whom he'd been married for thirty-four years, "I miss you, babe."

I hear you.

The second day, the conference didn't end until ten o'clock at night. And since we were three hours from home, we were supposed to stay another night at the hotel. But this guy? He's got us driving until one o'clock in the morning so that he does not have to spend another night away from his wife. I saw this man acting like he was in puppy love. I mean, he was a complete mess. And it blew my mind. I didn't even know people could act like that. A couple dating in high school? Sure. They're going to be sappy. But grown folks married more than three decades?

When we have these kinds of mentors in our lives, we see what marriage can be.

Mentors and Age

You already know that I want you dating in community, with people around you and the person you are dating. And I want you to solicit the opinions of people your age: your bestie, your siblings, your crew from church. But you also need older believers to weigh in.

Titus 2:4–6 encourages older women to take the younger women on and guide them. Paul challenged older men to take the younger men under their wing and lead them. If you don't yet have a person like that in your life—whether you're dating or not—start seeking a mentor now. Don't put it off.

Mentors and Gender

While mentors are usually older, wiser believers of the same gender as their mentee, I want to suggest a very specific way we can learn from mentors of the opposite gender.

I think every single man should have an older woman who can weigh in on the woman he's dating. Stay with me. I'm not saying that older men can't give you good counsel, but there's a real possibility that they could be *blinded*—like you could!—by a woman who's physically attractive. Or she bats her eyes, looking all cute. Or she's got a charming southern drawl. I promise you that a mature, spiritually discerning woman is going to have eyes to determine the character of the woman you're dating.

> She's asking, *Okay, honey, who are you?*
> She's wondering, *What are her intentions?*
> She's musing, *Is this a woman of character?*

You want the opinion of a maternal figure who will tell you the truth. I'm so grateful that my mom knew Zai. My mom has since passed, and maybe like me, you no longer have a maternal figure. But there is going to be an older woman at the church. Or a neighbor who loves God. Or an older sister.

And if you're a woman, you can invite an older man to spend time getting to know the man you're dating. Make space for him to do so.

When there are healthy boundaries, there is great value in having mentors of the opposite gender.

How do you find that person? It's really easy when you already have an older mentor who is married. Simply ask their spouse to weigh in on the person you are interested in. If you don't have an older mentor at all, I would encourage you to start serving at your church or join a small group—these are great ways to meet people you wouldn't normally encounter in your friend circles.

When you find that mentor of the opposite sex, ask them a million questions.

Ask them if the faith of the person you are interested in seems secure and mature.

Ask them if they see any pride, disrespectful tendencies, anger, or controlling temperaments that could be problematic down the road.

Ask them if they see maturity, a work ethic, a sober judgment of self and life.

Your Unsaved Parents

When I say that you need to date in community, I obviously mean you should do so while receiving counsel from these wise elders who can help you practice discernment. I'm talking about older adults who are submitted to God.

But let's talk about *parents* who are not. Even if your parents aren't saved, you should introduce the person you are dating to them. You don't necessarily need to introduce them in the first month of dating, but once things get serious, make space for your parents to get to know your partner. Sometimes we write off our parents because they don't believe in Jesus. But you know what? Your father is still supposed to be your protector. Whether he believes in Jesus or not. Your unsaved parents still have a biblical role to watch over your life.

And guess what? Many unbelieving fathers can spot a loser a mile away. An unbelieving mother can still discern it. Sometimes we can be tempted to write off our parents' opinions because their faith is not as strong as ours. Don't make that mistake.

If God can speak through a donkey (see Numbers 22), He can speak to your unsaved dad and your unsaved mom. I'm not calling your parents donkeys, but you get the idea. They may not know Jesus, but they likely know a jerk when they see one.

When You're Dating, You Need Mentors Above You: Indirect Mentoring

I was blessed to have a godly man I could look up to in my life. My parents also had a great marriage I could watch and learn from up close. The men and women who mentor us are gifts. But I also know that you might not have someone like this in your life right now. However, we can also learn and grow from those I'm going to call "indirect" mentors. Their help looks a little different, but don't despise their influence.

Indirect mentors include the godly older man whose podcast you eat up.

Or the wise woman whose books you read.

Even the dogs eat crumbs from the master's table. And if you're hungry, you don't need a whole loaf of bread. You can *work* with crumbs. "Work a crumb" is one of my favorite phrases. It comes from Matthew 15, when a woman told Jesus she didn't need a whole loaf of bread, which referred to His healing power. Just a crumb from Jesus would be enough to bring a desperately needed miracle to her daughter.

You're dropping gems on your podcast? I can work with those crumbs.

You're offering gold on your radio show? I can work with those crumbs.

You're espousing truth in that sermon on YouTube? I can work with those crumbs.

Receive the wisdom of these voices as the indirect mentors God can still use to speak into your life.

Who Pursues Who?

If you don't have an older, trusted spiritual adviser, you need to find one.

Over the years I've known a lot of young adults who *needed* to be mentored. And many were *open* to being mentored. Some even desperately *wanted* to be mentored. But mentors weren't pursuing that kind of a relationship with them. So, they just accepted the fact that they weren't going to be mentored.

I'm pushing back on that mindset.

I think that the biblical precedent is that the mentee pursues the mentor.

In his letter to the early church in Corinth, Paul challenged the believers, "Follow my example, as I follow the example of Christ."[1] Paul was just walking it out and said it's the mentee's job to keep up.

We can also look at Elijah and Elisha. Their relationship began with Elijah seeing something great in the life of Elisha. Once Elisha was anointed by Elijah, he left his parents' home to follow Elijah and become his servant. It was the ancient version of *The Apprentice*. He ran after him. So I'm suggesting that the mentee is the one who needs to get their hustle on to *follow* a mentor.

After meeting Pastor Wayne in Louisiana, I knew he had something special. I looked up to him and really admired the way he lived his life. I loved what God was doing through him, and I knew I wanted to be around that. So, when I found out he was going to be preaching at a church in Pittsburgh, I jumped in my car and drove four hours *to be his apprentice.* For real: I held his Bible and his briefcase. When I was with this man, I watched every area of his life.

I was looking at the way he interacted with his wife.

I asked questions about the way they handled their finances.

I took note of the way he navigated his career.

And when I was considering proposing to Zai? I brought Wayne and his wife, CeCe, up to Maryland under the guise of doing a leadership retreat for my team. I knew I wanted to propose to Zai soon, and I wanted them to be around her.

Do you see any red flags?

Do you see any troubling signs?

What do you think?

Clearly, I got their approval! Which I treasured. I strongly believed Zai was God's person for me, but marriage is a really major decision, so it was important to me to receive Wayne and CeCe's blessing for a couple of reasons. First, because when it comes to relationships with the opposite sex, none of us should trust ourselves to make wise decisions on our own.[2] We need community; we need wise counsel from trusted friends; we need people who are willing to speak truth into our lives. Second, Wayne's counsel deepened my confidence in pursuing marriage with Zai. Input and counsel from people like Wayne contributed to a firm foundation for my marriage.

It had been the same with Pastor Carlos, who I drove with

when he was speaking at a church in Virginia. When I'd seen him doing student ministry in the Maryland area, I just knew I wanted to be around him. So I started showing up at that student ministry early to help them set up, and I stayed late to help them tear down. I didn't even go to church there, but I pursued the person I wanted to be around. The person I wanted to learn from.

Professionals who want to advance in their careers already *know* to do this. They do it in the business world. In real estate. In law. In medicine. Somehow, in those spheres, we understand that pursuing mentors is going to help us get what we want out of life, but too often we fail to do it when it comes to building a healthy relationship.

Take your next step, today, to pursue that godly older adult whose life you respect and from whom you want to learn.

When Do You Need These Mentors?

Single friend, post-engagement is *not* the time to parade your betrothed past the mentors who matter in your life. Nah, that needs to happen on the front end. Start seeking counsel from trusted mentors long before you pop the question. You want and need these people to sign off *before* you get engaged. Men, do not propose to someone who hasn't spent time around the older mentors you trust. Women, do not say yes to marrying someone your trusted people have not been around.

My mama was my spiritual protection. She hooked me up. If you don't have one, get yourself a wise spiritual overseer.

Now that you know how to travel *smart,* I want to walk you through the sequential phases of the road map to marriage: the spying phase, the talking phase, the dating phase, and engagement. (I'll even coach you through the "ending it" phase— which is sometimes exactly the right move.)

We'll start with the spying phase, which is not at all as creepy as it sounds.

Be Wary of These Messages Around Premarital Sex

Consensual sex in a loving dating relationship is permissible.

Situationships are normal.

Why would you buy a car without test-driving it?

We don't need a piece of paper to be committed to each other.

Spiritual marriages (a modern form of common-law marriage) are acceptable.

Love is love.

Pay Attention to Other Drivers

The Spying Phase of Dating

BEFORE I EVER ASKED ZAI OUT, I WANTED TO GET A SENSE OF WHO she was—her character, pursuits, dreams, and passions.

And as I watched, I saw how she walked in love.

When I first met Zai, she had a tight group of friends. Even among a pretty large group, I saw how Zai stood out. She was so selfless with her friends. I noticed how she served them, even though they couldn't always serve her back. I watched how she looked out for their best interests, even when it was extremely inconvenient.

And I thought, *If that's how she treats people who are just friends and not even family, imagine how she's going to treat her husband.*

It seemed as if I had found a good thing.

Spying Out the Land

In the Old Testament (Numbers 13–14), God promised Abraham that He would provide a home, a promised land, for His people. Well, Moses sent twelve spies to scout out the land of Canaan, checking it out as a future home for the Israelites. Moses asked them to scope out the land's geography. He wanted to know about the people who lived there. He was curious about what the agriculture was like. He wanted to know what the cities were like. He wanted these spies to bring back samples of what farmers were growing.

I'm gonna cut to the chase and tell you that ten of the twelve spies came back with a bad report, throwing shade on the land they'd seen. Only two of those spies who'd been sent—Joshua and Caleb—came back with a good report and the confidence that God would help them and give them the land.

Before you ever date someone, I want you to spy out the land. This is the first step in the dating process I'm about to unpack. You should do this before you ever ask someone out on a date or agree to a date. When you're spying out the land, you're observing someone in their natural habitat, the way I had my eye on Zai. You've seen that on Animal Planet, right? You get to peek at a species in the wild. You are not being creepy or overbearing; you are just observing them and learning about how they operate in their everyday life as the two of you interact. You're that field observer who's collecting data.

What do they do when they win at cards?
What do they do when they lose at Monopoly?
How does he celebrate the holidays?

What's she like with her friends?

How does he treat someone who's not valuable to him because they can't "do something" for him?

When you're on this dating adventure, you are not a tourist. You're a *spy*. The first step in dating is *not* asking someone out or being asked out. The first step in dating is to spy out the land. On this dating journey, you are discerning the character of the man or woman you may be considering. Don't overanalyze them or hold them to an impossible standard; just observe how they live, and look for consistency.

Maybe when he's around his homeboys, he acts one way.

And when she's at church, she acts another way.

And on Instagram, she acts another way.

While these observations don't tell the full story, you can determine a lot about a person without ever dating them. When you survey the land, you're gathering information for the sake of *dating fewer people*. Yeah, I said that. Pastor Wayne said, "Stephen, listen to me carefully. Men who are intentional about fulfilling their destiny don't date a lot of people. They are very intentional about the people they date. And that's because they have spent time *observing* before they jump in feetfirst."

I'll bet there are people you've dated whom you wouldn't have gone out with if you had just spent about three more minutes thinking about it. If you had observed them before you said "Hey, girl," or before you said "Yes," you would have saved yourself a lot of time and maybe some disappointment too. And here's the thing that people don't realize: Singleness is one of the most important seasons of your life. *God uses your season of singleness to prepare you for marriage.*

Here are some suggestions for spying out the land:

1. Start in their social media feed.

You know I was serving as a senior pastor when I first laid eyes on Zai. She walked into church, and I was like, "Oh, mama, who is that?" So I started spying out the land, scrolling through her Instagram feed. I was about three years into her feed when I got a little excited with the scroll, swiped too fast, and liked one of her pictures. Rookie mistake. Pro tip: Make sure you don't like any pictures two years down the feed. But you can learn a lot by what someone will or won't post. Don't lurk, and don't overanalyze the person. Remember that their social media doesn't tell the full story of who they are. But it is part of the story.

2. Observe them in their natural habitat.

You ever been traveling on a highway and see these maniacs speeding and swerving between lanes, missing other cars by inches? If you're like me, you breathe a sigh of relief that you're not in the vehicle they're driving. When you're spying out the land, you're watching someone around their friends, family, co-workers, or church fam to determine if they are the kind of person you could see yourself traveling down the road with. You're not being overly critical, but you are taking notice of how they behave at church, at a restaurant, at the mall, or at a park.

3. Keep your mission on the low.

When people know that they're being observed, they put their best foot forward. The only problem is that you're not marrying someone's best foot. You're marrying both their feet. So, you need to see who they are. Keep it low-key. Make room for them to show their true colors.

4. Settle down.

When you're observing someone you might be interested in dating, you don't need to be flirting with them, because you don't yet know if they're worth the flirt. Keep it chill. You need to figure out first if this person is worth bringing your best flirting game.

5. Notice how they treat people.

How does this person treat others (especially people they don't "need")? I mean, sure, they're going to be shiny and nice to their boss or to the pastor—or to you!—but when you're out with a larger group, how do they treat the person who's bussing tables at the restaurant? How do they treat the person who's taking tickets at the movie theater? How do they interact with the person outside the theater who's asking for spare change?

6. Determine if they're moving forward.

We've already established that this person doesn't need to be a millionaire—yet—or drive a Mercedes. But is there any evidence in this person's life that they're making progress on the goals they have for themselves, personally or professionally?

7. Pay attention to how they relate to the opposite sex.

You can glean some good intel by paying attention to the way this person interacts with the opposite sex. Homegirl got dudes around her all the time? Is he swarmed by honeys? "Nah, he's just a friend. And he's just a friend. And that other guy—just a friend." "Oh, her? A friend. And her? Just a friend. And she's a friend too." Let's be honest: If someone is not emotionally whole, they *need* the affirmation of all these different people.

And, no, they're not gonna date them; that doesn't matter. Come on, sister, I'm gonna be your pastor for a second: He doesn't *need* to have a female as his best friend.

When you're spying out the land, you're gathering intelligence on who this person is when they think nobody's watching. Don't skip this first step in the dating journey.

Now, if you meet on a dating app or through a mutual friend, it will obviously be hard to keep your interest private, but the same principle applies. Hopefully based on your search criteria or the credibility of your friend's endorsement, some of the "spying" has been done for you already. Still, move slow. Talk on the phone. Meet in public places, and get to know their community of friends as soon as possible. You want to get a good sense of who the person is before you start dating exclusively.

Make a Move

And you know that the spying has a purpose, right? The purpose is to gather enough information to decide whether to take the next step with this person. And the next step is a date.

Guys, you've vetted her as best you can, and she seems decent and sane, so ask her out. Say, "Hey, I like you. Would you like to go somewhere?" Where? Anywhere. I'm just saying, guys, state your business for the ladies.

Ladies, listen to me. Don't put up with a man who is going to string you along but never define the relationship. If he pays for your dinner, takes you out to the movies, and insists, "Oh, no, she's just my sister in Christ," I want you to push back. Because that whole "sister and brother in Christ" thing? If you don't have the same parents, he ain't your brother. That's just weird and awkward. Somebody likes somebody, and the other person doesn't want to admit it.

Women, men don't value what they don't pursue. Let them pursue you so that they will value you. But don't play hard to get. Don't be surrounded by your homegirls twenty-four hours a day, like you got Secret Service protecting you. When you're always in the company of your girls, you're making it harder for him to come over and say, "Hi, Jayla."

Unfortunately, what I see too often when people are dating is that they play games.

I'm playing hard to get.
I'm not going to call him.
I'm going to give him three days.
She's got to call me because last time I called her.
I was the last one to text, and everybody knows you don't double text. You just wait.
I'm not going over there.

Those are games. Women, don't play games. Men, don't play games. If you've spied out the land, and you like what you've seen, it's time to handle your business. It's time to shift gears and enter the *talking* phase of dating.

More Corny Pickup Lines

"Hey, girl. You must be from Memphis, because you're the only ten I see."

"I was reading in the book of Numbers, and I realized I don't have yours."

"I'm not an expert at math, but I'm great with numbers. How about this, you give me yours and just wait to see what I can do with it?"

"Do I know you from somewhere?" (#WorksLikeACharm)

Communicate with Other Drivers

The Talking Phase of Dating

WHEN ZAI AND I WERE DATING, SHE USED TO WORK NIGHTS AT A hospital. So one morning, I woke up at like 5:00 A.M. She lived and worked in southern Maryland, and I lived about an hour away. So, I jumped in the car and drove to her workplace.

I put a big bushel of roses on her windshield, with a love note, in the hospital parking lot for her to see when she got off work.

Zai *loved* it.

But I wasn't dropping roses off in the early morning after our first date. And, if I'm honest, I'm not dropping roses *every week* now that we're married. Relationships have different phases, and I want you to know how to navigate them wisely.

Talking

After you've spied out the land, the first stage in getting to know someone is *talking* (or at least that's what folks a lot younger than me call it). But let's make sure we're on the same page about what this means. The kind of communication that happens in this early phase of a relationship can include:

- Messaging on a dating app
- Texting
- Talking on the phone
- Video chats
- Doing stuff with groups

The talking stage is when you're getting to know someone and you're not yet exclusive. In fact, it's possible to be talking to more than one person—with *integrity*.

But let's pause right there. At *integrity*. Make sure you're both on the same page. Brother, if you've saved her as "Sis" in your phone and she's got you saved as "Papi" in hers, y'all might not be on the same page. She's ready to take your last name, and you *know* you're not that interested. That kind of talking is sinful—you're knowingly leading somebody on. If you're unsure whether the two of you are on the same page, that's one thing, but once you know you are not interested, you are responsible to honor and respect the person you are talking to. This means checking yourself and your behavior so you don't lead them on.

What to Look For

In the talking stage, the first things you want look for are major red flags: signs of emotional, mental, physical, or spiritual unhealthiness. If someone is particularly unhealthy in one or more of these ways, pay attention. Use wisdom.

In this early stage, you're also looking for *chemistry*. I'm going to say that's a combination of these same four things! It's about emotional, mental, physical, and spiritual attraction. It's how you vibe when you're together.

Emotional Attraction

When you're emotionally attracted to someone, you might find yourself noticing . . .

> I can just be myself around them.
> I'm transparent with this person.
> I'm able to share all of who I am.
> I'm able to be entirely honest.
> I find myself saying stuff that I wouldn't say around other
> people.

Mental Attraction

I've heard women say that they're attracted to a man's mind. Um . . . I don't even know what that means. As a guy, that sounds strange to me. But I think they might be saying something like, "I love the way he dreams." Or, "I love the way he thinks." Or, "I love the way he problem solves." Or, "I love the way he communicates." They might just be saying, "This person fascinates me."

Physical Attraction

I don't need to tell you what this is. You're on your own. Just know it is important. Forever is a long time. Some Christians get too spiritual and don't think looks should factor in. Looks certainly are not the most important thing, and there better be more than just physical attraction that draws you to the person. However, God gave you eyes for a reason, and the Bible is intentional in sometimes describing a woman's beauty or a man's handsomeness. I want to give you permission to look for someone you find physically attractive. In fact, pursuing someone you really don't find physically attractive is misleading.

Spiritual Attraction

I've heard single people say some weird stuff.

> When he prays, I feel closer to Jesus.
> Her love for the Word just does it for me.
> His prayer life is so inspiring.

Okay, go take a cold shower. Pull yourself together. Do we want to see that someone loves God? Yes. For sure. But you are not going to marry every person who can pray a good prayer. This said, you do want to keep your eyes open for someone who's submitted to God. Look for evidence that they are actively pursuing Jesus and that their relationship with Him influences their decision-making. Look for someone who not only attends church but also actively serves. Someone who cares for their community and seeks accountability.

What to Avoid in the Talking Phase

When you're in that early talking phase, you gotta keep it light. The first time you grab coffee with someone, you don't need to decide between a three-bedroom home and a four-bedroom one. You probably also don't need to share all your past trauma in the first few dates. Dial it back.

Folks often get in trouble when they go too deep too fast, *together*. (Even if it's mutual, that doesn't make it right.) If you both inch toward that kind of intimacy together, you might fool yourselves into thinking it's right. It's magical. It's destiny.

Nope. It's foolish.

When you're talking to someone, you don't need to know how many children he hopes to have one day. You don't need to know her ring size. Settle down. When you're in that talking phase, stay in your lane.

You like chocolate?
Gryffindor or Hufflepuff?
Did you play sports in high school? Which ones?
Favorite musician?

While there aren't any hard-and-fast rules, I'm going to suggest that this talking phase doesn't need to last more than twelve weeks. Even that's long, but I'm giving grace for my more indecisive friends. You're not choosing baby names or looking for side-by-side burial plots.

You're looking for red flags. Yellow flags.

You're seeing if you have chemistry.

By twelve weeks, you know what you need to know. Longer than that? You're playing with that person's heart.

If You're Doing It Right, It's a Win-Win

After you've engaged in talking, you need to fish or cut bait. And I'm going to say that if you've done it well, this is a win-win situation. If you're feeling this person, and you haven't seen any red flags, then that's a win. You end up dating.

If there's something that signals that you shouldn't move forward with this person, that experience of getting to know them can still be a win.

When I dated a girl I'll call Pam, we spent time together going to the theater. When we went to see *The Screwtape Letters,* it was the first time I'd ever seen a live play. We had a blast checking out different shows together. And even though we never officially dated and ended up going our separate ways after a few weeks of *talking,* I still fondly remember the fun we had. It was my introduction to a world I hadn't encountered before.

So, if you're not crossing moral boundaries when you are talking to or dating someone, even when it doesn't work out, it can be a win. You can grow by learning about yourself, the other person, and the world.

Talking Is Just Talking

You move wisely, in dating, when you move through these phases intentionally. If you're talking, it means you've spied out the land and you like what you see. As you talk, you glean even more information about this person. If you're seeing green lights, it's time to date.

Q: Should I climb into his or her DMs?

A: Absolutely! There is nothin wrong with messaging someone and commenting on their location, food, statements, and so on. But I would avoid commenting on their looks and physical features, as that could come across as you just trying to smash. It could signal you're simply interested in having sex and not looking to pursue a real godly relationship.

Q: Does a guy or girl have to have their money in order before dating?

A: Don't despise small beginnings; do despise small endings. You do need to have enough money to be able to pay for dinner, gas, and maybe flowers, but—if you're a student—you don't have to have a full-time job, be wealthy, and be debt-free before you start dating. You should be more concerned about whether he has a vision and a plan to build a great life than about what money he makes. There is nothing wrong with dating in college when you are both unemployed but are in a place that will hopefully lead to full-time employment.

Use Your Signals

The Dating Phase of Dating

LET'S TALK ABOUT THAT FIRST DATE. GUYS, I'M TALKING TO YOU right now. And, ladies, you get to listen in. (You're welcome.)

Men, you know what a first date can be like. You go to pick her up, and you're sweating before you get to the door. Then you see her, all put together—dolled up and wearing makeup—and that doesn't help. You're still sweating. She's at a *distinct* advantage.

Guys, I'm giving you permission right now to level the playing field. Specifically, I'm suggesting that you share an experience that will throw her off-balance a little. (Because even in those heels, she is not off-balance.) I'm talking about an ice-skating rink. Or a roller-skating rink. When she's got those skates on and is just trying to keep from falling over, she's not thinking too much about making you sweat. I'm not suggest-ing anything shady; I'm just offering a way to level the playing field. Slick surfaces don't necessarily have to be involved. Maybe you go bowling, apple picking, or miniature golfing. Maybe you take her to a cooking class. You're welcome.

First Season of Dating: Have Fun

For the first six to twelve weeks of dating, just enjoy yourself. (And to be clear, "Netflix and chill" is not what I mean.) Have fun, because it doesn't need to get serious that early. No one needs to be talking about what flavor wedding cake they want or what their net worth is. Settle down. Have fun, and enjoy each other's company. You'll be shocked at the level of honesty and transparency you can get from someone when you're hav-ing fun. In this season, your emotional, physical, spiritual, and mental attraction either will be confirmed or will dissipate.

One of the best dates Zai and I ever had was when we went to D.C., rented those dollar bikes, and rode around the monuments. Neither of us had ridden a bike in over ten years, and we had a blast (even though I was outrageously out of shape).

Second Season of Dating: Look for Unity of Vision

In the second season of dating, check to see if you have unity of vision. If you've begun dating, you've agreed that there's something you see in the other person—emotionally, mentally, physically, spiritually—that you respect. As you move into that second season, take a harder look at where this person's life is headed.

Do you want to go there?

If you're a woman, can you submit to him for the rest of your life?[1] (Yeah, it just got real. This is so much heavier than Monopoly.)

When I was dating Zai, I knew I was going to be in ministry for the rest of my life, so I couldn't marry a woman who didn't have a heart for ministry. One of the questions I asked while we were dating was "Does she love the church?" I knew that I loved the church and would be in it for the rest of my life. If I married someone who didn't, I knew we'd both be in trouble. I knew the type of woman I needed because of God's call on my life.

In this second season of dating, determine if you share a unified vision.

How Long Should We Date?

If you're planning to move toward marriage, you should not date for less than six months. (Do as I say, not as I do.) I know Zai and I only dated for twelve weeks before getting engaged, but we had been friends and in the same orbit for two years prior. Even then, in hindsight it wouldn't have been bad for us to date for another three to six months before getting engaged. If you're rushing toward engagement? That's a red flag. Danger! Danger! Proceed with extreme caution.

If you date for less than twelve months, you ain't seen this person go through a winter yet. I'm just saying . . . it gets dark at five o'clock. Seasonal depression is real. Now, I don't suffer from clinical seasonal depression, but I'm a lot happier when spring comes around. I'm outside playing with the kids at seven o'clock in the evening. You want to see your beloved in every season.

At one level, I'm playing. But you actually do want to see people in *every* season.

How does he respond to an offense?

How does she weather disappointment?

How does he navigate illness?

How does she celebrate?

How does he respond to criticism?

You want to see it all.

My suggestion: You probably don't want to date for much less than twelve months, and I also want to recommend that you don't date for longer than two years.

That's. Just. More. Red. Flags. Neither rushing into marriage nor perpetually putting it off is going to help you flourish.

How many people have invested five years into a relationship that ended in a devastating breakup? That's five years of delaying the amazing marriage God has for you. That's five years of making life decisions while considering someone who ultimately will not be there when that decision comes to fruition. That's five years of moving toward someone as your potential life partner, only to watch them walk away. The breakup will feel almost like a divorce. The struggle to trust again, open up again, fully commit again, will be exponentially more difficult and painful. It's just not worth it. Be intentional, and guard your heart.

I know I'm stepping on some toes now. If you know someone who dated for five years and is now in an amazing marriage, I know you want to fight me. Sure, there are exceptions to the rule. But it's a *rule* for a reason.

I'm thinking of one couple who dated for four years. They knew they wanted to marry, but he was in residency on one side of the country and she was in law school on the other. They didn't want to be married until they could be in the same city to start their lives together. This is a perfectly reasonable exception to the rule.

While you don't want to drag your feet, give yourself enough time to see this person in all kinds of seasons and situations. And if you've been dating for a long time and find yourself putting off marriage for minor reasons, that's probably a sign you need to consider whether it's time to call things off. Clear is kind. Live with integrity, and remember that the person you are dating is made in God's image—strive to treat them with the utmost respect.

Let's Keep It Real

If you're ready to move past the talking phase, you are undoubtedly attracted to each other. This next stage is the one where every time you hold their hand, you feel butterflies. Or when you wake up and the first thing you see is a text message from them, your heart thrills. You're thinking, *They're so sleek.* You don't even pay your rent anymore because all you can do is think about that person. You're useless.

You're in the attraction stage.

The infatuation stage.

The fantasy stage.

The honeymoon period (which may precede the actual honeymoon but hopefully lasts long enough to get you there).

That attraction is *biology.* And, scientifically, endorphins are preventing you from seeing anything negative about that other person. You're focused on what you share in common, and you're ignoring that person's flaws. You're only seeing the good in them. There is little or no conflict in this stage. You can't even *think of anything to fight about!* Experts say this stage lasts anywhere from three months to two years. Hear me: It's not a bad stage. In fact, it's really fun. But . . . it won't last forever.

When the Honeymoon Is Over

At some point—even if this is the person God has for you!—the feels are going to fade. At some point, you're going to start to see the chinks in the armor of your beloved. It's not that you're no longer in love, but your partner doesn't seem as great as he or she once did.

> She talks a lot.
> He smells funny.
> They're cheap.
> Why don't they have more ambition?

Remember those endorphins that were keeping you from seeing the flaws in the other person? Well, your body can't do that forever. And when those endorphins decrease, the rose-colored glasses come off. The next thing you know, you're thinking, *I don't know if this person is who I thought they were* . . .

Pay attention! That is where you want to be!

In the legit dating phase of dating, pay attention to the signals the other person is giving out. Dating is about communicating who you are to each other.

This—this period after the endorphins have settled down when you're able to see your partner's flaws—is the *only* stage when you want to move toward engagement. It's the only stage when you should make long-term decisions and commitments because reality has started to kick in. The very best engagement decisions I've seen people make are when they're in this stage. They've seen the other's flaws, but the benefits of their strengths outweigh those flaws. The other person is never going to change, *significantly,* from who they are in this stage. So, you need to be fully committed to who they are, flaws and all.

Have Fun, and Be Wise

When you start dating, have fun. Enjoy getting to know each other. And when you get a bit more serious, evaluate whether you and this person have a unity of vision. If you do? It might just be time to take the next step.

Oh yeah, we're going there . . .

Great Dates

1. Go roller-skating.
2. Have fun bowling.
3. Restaurant hop to different places for apps, a main course, and dessert.
4. Try axe throwing.
5. Go canoeing.
6. Take a cooking class.
7. Go apple picking.
8. Hike and picnic.
9. Go ice-skating.
10. Build a fire and roast marshmallows.
11. Take a dance class.
12. Sing karaoke.

13. Volunteer together.
14. Go rock climbing.
15. Visit the zoo.
16. See a play at the theater.
17. Go out to a jazz club.
18. Explore a museum.
19. Zip around the city on rented bikes or scooters.
20. Take a painting class.
21. Attend a basketball game.
22. Go to a water park.

Choose a Co-Pilot

The Engagement Phase of Dating

WHEN ZAI AND I WERE DATING, I RECRUITED HER TO HELP PLAN my twenty-sixth birthday party. She thought it was super weird to make such a big deal of *twenty-six*.

But that's because she didn't yet know that it would actually be an *engagement* party.

We rented out the community center of a brand-new apartment building that was just amazing. We invited our closest friends to be with us. Sadly, my mom's cancer was too far advanced for her to attend, but she watched on FaceTime.

With everyone watching, I got down on one knee—in front of Zai's mom and sister—and read Zai the last poem she would receive for the next decade. Speechless, all she could do was cry. We hugged and took pictures and celebrated with our loved ones. I knew she loved poetry, and on that night, I made her believe I was a poet.

Yeah, I totally tricked her into marrying me.

Pulling the Trigger

Once you've been dating someone long enough to confirm you're attracted to each other, there aren't any red flags and any yellow flags can be addressed, you have a shared vision, you've observed them in various situations, and you've gained the approval of your trusted mentors . . . then it's time.

Guys, it's simple. You ask her to marry you.

Ladies, you don't need to wait on him forever. Make him ask that question. Give him an ultimatum. (I don't mean be manipulative. I mean, if he's tarrying, let him know he needs to handle his business.)

There are 1,001 reasons to put off an engagement. You want to graduate first. (Respect.) You want to have money in the bank. (Mad respect.) You want to have your life in order. You want to be able to buy the perfect engagement ring. I love something Dave Ramsey said: "The size of a diamond on an engagement ring does not indicate the future success of a marriage."[1]

Four-carat diamonds have led to marriages that ended in divorce, and cheap rings have led to amazing sixty-year marriages.

Boom.

The same can be said for all the other details of your life that you want to have in order. The impulse is not a bad one, but most of these details shouldn't be deal-breakers when it comes to moving toward the altar.

Do the best with what you have, where you are.

What Happens in the Engagement Phase

The engagement phase of dating is for finalizing unity and vision. (Sure, sure, you're planning a potentially massive social event for a host of people you like and don't like. There's that too.) The engagement period is the time to start having major conversations about what your married life will look like. Specifically, you need to cultivate a unified vision for faith, family, finances, the future, and healthy life rhythms. (I wanted to say *fitness* for that last one to keep my alliteration, but it didn't quite work.)

These are conversations you can't not have during your engagement.

FAITH

Where do we intend to worship?
What will our personal relationships with God look like?
How will we come before the Lord together?
How will our faith be lived out in the world?
Do we intend on tithing no matter the season of life?

FAMILY

When would we like to grow our family by having children?
How many children do we hope to have?
Will we consider adoption?
How will we parent together?
What values will guide our parenting?
How will we care for our larger family (such as our parents in old age)?

FINANCES

What kind of debt is each of us bringing to the marriage?

What are our plans for paying off that debt?

Will we both work?

Will both of us continue working once we have children?

What are our expectations about how we will spend money?

How will we save for the future?

How will we give our money? How will we prioritize generosity?

FUTURE

While we can't control what happens, how do we imagine the decades unfolding?

Do we plan to stay where we are geographically, or are we open to moving?

Do we hope to own a home? If so, how will we plan for that?

Do we envision retirement? If so, how will we plan financially for that?

How will we navigate, together, the unexpected?

HEALTHY LIFE RHYTHMS

Do either of us have a propensity to overcommit to work and schedule obligations?

How will we prioritize and protect quality time together?

If one or both of us already live with physical challenges, or expect to in the future, how will we manage those?

How will we ensure that we are both emotionally healthy? How will we encourage each other's emotional, mental, and spiritual health?

When the hurts from our past bubble up and interfere
with our relationships, what's our plan?

What about social health? How will each of us navigate
our individual and shared friendships once we're married?

How do each of us plan to stay physically fit and healthy?

The purpose of these conversations is to find unity. If
you're not getting there, slow it down. Talk to your mentors,
and get insight from people you trust. It might take some work
to reach a shared vision on one of these topics. The time you
put into this work is worth it.

What You Can Expect During Engagement

What you can expect during engagement will be determined
in part by what is coming after. And what comes next is a
commitment to a lifelong marriage with God as the foundation.

"Husbands, love your wives, just as Christ loved the
church."[2] "Wives, submit yourselves to your own husbands as
you do to the Lord."[3] Do you hear it? Marriage is a picture of
how God loves His church and how the church loves God.

The devil ain't celebrating your engagement. *The Enemy
hates marriage.* We know this. As you're moving through these
phases toward marriage, you're moving toward what the Enemy
detests. So, you can *expect* spiritual warfare.

Sudden health crisis? Don't be surprised.

Fired from your job the day after you propose? Yeah, that
tracks.

In-laws putting pressure on who makes the guest list? Get
behind us, Satan.

Friend, just plan on *all* that mess.

You think that sexual temptation is gonna ramp up during your engagement period? Plan on that too. You can bet there are a lot of couples who remained pure and then rationalized sleeping together once they were engaged. "But we love each other." "But we're committed to each other." "We're gonna get married." Is this you? If so . . . *You've made it this far. You're almost to the finish line. Don't give in now.*

We've all seen that Instagram video of the athlete who was out in front of the whole pack of competitors, inches away from winning the race, when they tripped and fell right before the finish line. Yeah . . . don't do that. Engagement is not your "get out of jail free" card for sleeping together before you're married. (Because, as you know, what you do before marriage has consequences for your marriage.) Think of your engagement as preparation for marriage. One of the ways you prepare for marriage during engagement is by striving to live with integrity and exercise self-control—two character traits that are crucial to a healthy marriage.

Don't stumble before you reach the finish line.

Still Not Convinced?

I want to make sure that we're on the same page about this "waiting" thing. Because maybe you're still not convinced. Maybe you're thinking, *Pastor, you don't know how hard it is.* Well, I actually do, but let's come at it from another direction.

Somebody who is pressuring you to have sex with them is someone who does not respect your relationship with God. Sin affects our closeness to God. It doesn't keep Him from loving us, but it does affect our ability to run to Him and hear Him when He speaks to us. Sin creates distance.

Here's the math: More than half of U.S. Christians believe that casual sex before marriage is sometimes or always acceptable.[4] About 80 percent of people—in church!—who are heading toward the altar have not remained virgins before marriage. I mention that to say that there is a very good chance that whoever you marry thought this way at some point. There is a good chance the person you want to marry is not a virgin. In other words, you're entering into marriage with a deficit. You're not even at zero—you're at negative twenty-five. I don't say this to condemn you; it's just reality.

Don't start marriage with a deficit.

The Way You Start: A Caution

I want you to move through this process in an orderly way: spying, talking, dating, engagement, marriage. I also know that it's not always that simple.

Maybe you didn't wait for marriage to have sex.

Maybe you moved in together before marriage.

Maybe he never really popped the question.

Maybe you had four kids together.

But . . . you got saved! You're in church now! You have a godly marriage! And it all worked out.

I gotta call foul on that. Not because I have any interest in judging you but because I care about you. I want you to know that you are going to have to deal with issues in your marriage that you would not have to deal with if you'd had a better start. Just because you survived the shipwreck doesn't mean the shipwreck was God's best for you. I need you to know that if your relationship started off in a way that wasn't the healthiest—for you or your spouse—you have some work to do. You will have to rebuild your transparency and honesty with God and perhaps with each other too. You will have to learn how to build a healthy intimacy that is not based in taking but in serving. You will have to find freedom from shame that sometimes shows up as a constant sense of being overlooked or forgotten. God is in the business of moving marriage into something that is beautiful, fulfilling, and beyond anything you can dream, but you must surrender yourself and your marriage to Him. No matter your past, a marriage submitted to God takes time and intentionality. You are going to have to put in a lot of work and endure some difficult seasons.

Prepare for Marriage

Even if your relationship during dating was pure, there are plenty of other things to work on during engagement. It may not need to be said, but I do hope you'll choose to get premarital counseling from your pastor. While that's going to look a little different for different pastors and different couples, it's so important.

Premarital counseling gives you the opportunity to confirm, in the presence of a spiritual leader you trust, that you're both on the same page about faith, family, finances, the future, and the healthy life rhythms you hope to build. Premarital counseling does not guarantee a healthy marriage, but it does help you prepare for one. A good premarital counselor will ask hard questions that you hadn't previously considered and will help you make sure you are ready for the lifelong commitment of marriage.

It's going to give you an extra layer of accountability to stay pure until marriage. (Or, if you haven't stayed pure until marriage, it will give you a chance to recalibrate and make better choices.)

It's going to help you uncover the kinds of challenges you might face in marriage and think through how to deal with them.

It's going to provide a space where you can work on your communication skills with each other. And, I promise you, there is work to be done.

Learn Marriage Skills

Rarely do people leave their childhood homes with a healthy understanding of how to deal with conflict. Rarely does anyone leave with a solid understanding of how to meet the needs of somebody who's completely different than they are. How do I know this? While Zai and I certainly had to figure a lot of this out ourselves, I've also seen it countless times while meeting with engaged couples for premarital counseling.

Now, I know I'm going to get some blowback on this, but the bestseller *The 5 Love Languages* by Gary Chapman has confused more people than you can imagine. Don't get me wrong, aspects of the book are amazing, and the concept that we all communicate and receive love in different ways is priceless. However, it's problematic because it can lead you to believe that if your spouse does not express love in the particular way you receive love, they don't love you. I just want to push back and say that it is more likely that they do love you, deeply, but they just haven't learned to speak your language yet. Remember that love is patient and kind.[5]

For example, one of my love languages is receiving gifts. On the other hand, the way Zai experiences love is through words of affirmation. And if I had understood that when we got married? I would have saved a lot of money over the years!

It turns out that sharing thoughtful words on a card is a *lot* cheaper than a new pair of red-soled heels. I was buying her gifts—which is one of the ways I experience and receive love— and what she needed was words of affirmation.

I hadn't yet learned to speak her language.

One of the most important marriage skills you can begin to learn during your engagement is healthy communication.

Make Your Engagement Season Count

Back in the day, before GPS, you had to rely on a road atlas, a huge folded-up map, or a printout of the directions you needed to get where you were going. And as hazardous as it is today to check your texts when you're driving, I promise you that it was just not possible to safely navigate your journey, and choose the right exit, while driving solo back then. If you were lucky, you had a co-pilot. You had that person in the seat next to you who had your back and was reading the map. And the two of you would get there together. Engagement is when you begin to learn what it's like to navigate life with this other person at your side.

Honestly, too many people assume that the engagement period is about the dress, the flowers, the seating chart, and the cake. It's not. It's about laying the best foundation you can for the life you plan to build together. Make the most of it.

Okay . . . it's about to get real . . .

At any point in this natural progression toward marriage— spying out the land, talking, dating, or engagement—you could come to the realization that the person you're getting to know is *not* the one God has for you. And when you realize that, it is time to locate the nearest exit ramp.

Rom-Coms to Convince Us That Love Conquers All

1. *Crazy Rich Asians*
Takeaway: Love conquers all. (Even tricky families.)
2. *The Wedding Planner*
Takeaway: Love conquers all. (Even engagements.)
3. *Love Actually*
Takeaway: Love conquers all. (Even class differences.)

Kick a Hitchhiker to the Curb

The "Ending It" Phase of Dating

"GOD TOLD ME WHO MY WIFE IS GOING TO BE."

That was me. At sixteen. Standing in front of our church. Being all bold about "God told me who my wife is going to be." It was a young lady I was dating at the time.

Now, I didn't say her name, but . . . it was a seventy-five-member church. They absolutely knew who I was talking about. I'd started dating a girl, and I was pretty sure she'd become my wife. She was fifteen, and we dated for two years.

Now, my mother *knew* that this girl was not the one. My mother also knew how stubborn I was. She reasoned, "If I tell him not to date her, he'll date her for another three years." So, she didn't do that. What she did was sneakier.

I shared with you that in my freshman year of college, she

told me, "Stephen, I'm pretty much the same woman I was when I was sixteen."

Now, I knew who my mother was, and I understood what she was saying.

"I'm a lot more godly," she continued. "But I was loud then, and I'm loud now."

What she was sneaky-saying to me was, "If you're waiting for this girl to change, she's not going to change. She is who she is."

Clever, right?

And what ultimately caused me to break up with her, when I was eighteen, was this thought: *I'm not excited about this woman raising my kids. I'm not excited about my future daughter turning out like her.* I don't say that to be harsh—she was a lovely person in many ways—but that was my honest assessment.

If you're a woman, do you want the man you're dating to raise your son? Do you want your son to grow up to be like him? If you don't want your future children to be shaped by this person, to become like them, then you shouldn't attach yourself to them.

Despite my bold and brazen announcement in the house of God that I'd found my wife, the right thing to do—the faithful thing—was to break it off. My goodness, was I embarrassed. I had that nauseous feeling in my stomach for a few weeks after. I felt like a sad country song for a bit, but I survived.

And I want you to hear that if the person you're dating isn't the kind of person you'd like your children to become, or if they're not listening to God and being transformed by Him, you have permission to call it off.

If you've been on one date, you have permission to call it off.

If you've been dating for nine months, you have permission to end it.

If you're engaged, you have permission to *not marry* the person you thought you were going to marry. It's better to be embarrassed and nauseous for a season than miserable for a lifetime.

So, let's dish about ending a relationship.

If you're talking to someone and discern it's not the right relationship for you, you can gently end the friendship.

If you're dating someone and realize that this is not a person you could build a life with? Break up.

And if it's the night before the wedding and you finally want to heed the cautions your mentors have been sharing throughout your relationship? You have permission to not marry that person.

Wherever you are in your journey—before you get hitched—you have permission to call it off. Maybe you look at the person beside you and you realize, *Oh no, this is not my co-pilot. This is a hitchhiker, and they've got to go!* It will take courage to break it off, but you can do it.

If you're not seeing your co-pilot, you've *got* to do it.

When Ending It Crushes You

I know it's not easy to break off a relationship that seemed promising. When you do, I want you to notice whether you experience disappointment or devastation. It is completely natural to feel deep disappointment when a relationship ends, whether it's after two weeks or two months or even two years.

But if you've dated someone for four months and the breakup leaves you feeling *devastated,* I want you to pay close attention to that. That feeling of devastation is telling you something you need to receive. If you lose forty pounds because you're not eating after a breakup with a guy you knew for four months, your body is telling you that there's a deeper problem you need to address. If you have to call in sick to work because you can't get out of bed, pay attention to that.

I'm going to suggest what's going on inside you when you're devastated in that way is actually not about the breakup. The breakup has magnified a deeper issue. There is a chance all your hopes and dreams were placed in a person and not rooted in Christ's plan and promise for your life. There's a chance that rejection and the fear of being alone forever has left you void of all hope. When you experience devastation, reach out for help and deal with what's at the root of that pain.

Yes, it might hurt. But what's worse than ending a relationship that's not right is continuing one.

Even Engagement Does Not Mean *You* Have to Get Married

The very best time to have a divorce is before you get married. If you're seeing red flags, even ones you didn't notice when you were dating, get out while you can. Maybe you realize the red flag is you; you're just not ready to commit to someone for a lifetime.

But I already posted the engagement announcement on Instagram . . .

But we already paid the caterer . . .

But we already sent out the invitations . . .

For too many couples, by the time they get to premarital counseling, the train is already barreling down the track. And it takes courage to ask, "Should we, or shouldn't we?"

Brother, sister, long after Insta and the caterer and the invitations are in the rearview but before you say "I do," you need to know for sure. "Should we, or shouldn't we?" Don't convince yourself that is not a question you can ask the night before the wedding. You *should* be asking it the night before the wedding. It might be devasting to your fiancé to call it off at such a late stage, but clear is kind.

Let's say you wake up on the morning of your wedding day and you know that you should not be marrying the person with whom you intend to make lifelong vows.

Cold feet are not uncommon. It perfectly natural to feel uncertain or nervous about this massive, life-altering decision. But I am not talking about cold feet.

Maybe your family has been expressing concerns and you've been ignoring them.

Maybe you have a powerful communication from the Lord and you know you are *not* to marry this person.

Maybe your best friend, who is wise and faithful and kind, sat you down a week earlier to caution you against marrying this person for some really valid reasons.

Maybe this awakening comes completely out of the blue but when you run it past trusted advisers at 6 A.M. on wedding day, they confirm your intuition.

Can you imagine how humiliating it would be to leave the woman or man you planned to marry *at the altar*?

And yet, you don't owe anything to all the people who traveled to your wedding and wore their best clothes. You don't even owe a lifetime commitment to the person who offered you a ring, or accepted a ring you offered, if they are not the person you should marry.

Sometimes, Ending It Is Right

The purpose of dating is to find someone to marry. But at any point in the dating process—when you're talking or dating or engaged—you have permission to end the relationship if your gut, your God, and the advisers you trust are telling you it's not right.

Okay, we really had to talk about when and how to use the exit ramp, but let's return now to the road to marriage. If this is the road you're on, let's talk about how you know whether someone is the kind of traveling companion with whom you can go the distance. I'll start by offering the ladies an assessment tool.

Assess Him as a Traveling Companion

Ask These Four Questions

Note: This chapter is for the ladies.

HAVE YOU EVER TAKEN A *LONG* ROAD TRIP WITH SOMEONE? IF YOU have, you know that your traveling companion is going to determine whether that trip feels like a journey to the moon and back or whether the time flies by. And because the right music makes everything better, I honestly think that the most important person in the car is the one responsible for the playlist. Before you take off on the journey of a lifetime—#marriage— you should know that you know that you know the person you're marrying is the right one. So, I want to give you some tools to assess whether or not someone is the right traveling companion.

For example, let's say your cousin has been telling you about a guy she works with who would be perfect for you.

He's fine, he's employed, and his gramma took him to church when he was a boy. She asks you if she can give him your number, and she promises that he's a lot of fun and that you'll have a great time. And you wonder, *Is that enough? Is this someone I could even imagine journeying with?* You love that someone is thinking about your dating life, but you're wondering what you should be looking for if you talk or meet up.

Questions Women Should Ask

When you're dating, you're dating for a purpose. That purpose is marriage. So I want you to ask some strategic questions to determine if the man you're dating is marriage material.

Is He Sovereign or Submitted?

In my first job, I worked for an insurance company. I had a department head and also a team leader.

The department head had interviewed me for the job and hired me, and I was afraid of her. She was all about the numbers: Did you meet them or not? She didn't smile much, and she didn't talk to me much. We didn't have a lot of interaction, with the exception of my year-end report and my midyear evaluation. I sweated through those meetings, and I survived.

Then there was my team leader. She was more like, "You can do it! Keep on going. You stay late, you show up early, and you're going to do great!" Even though my team leader was my boss and could fire me, she operated more as my biggest encourager rather than my taskmaster.

She knew that she was also under authority and that my performance was a reflection on her. There's a difference between submitting to someone who is your boss and submitting to a fellow laborer who has been put over you by authority.

The Bible clearly teaches in Ephesians 5:22 that God has made the husband the head of the home, and wives are to "submit to your own husbands, as to the Lord" (NKJV). And if you're sucking your teeth right now, first of all, ladies, you get it easy. Wives are to submit to their husbands, but Ephesians 5 says husbands are to lay their lives down and die to their own desires for their wives.[1] In my opinion, submitting sounds better than dying. Not to mention, it's different submitting to a boss and submitting to another worker who is at the same level as you but has been placed over you by the boss. God has not made men superior to women, but He does hold the man accountable for the well-being of his wife as he allows God to direct him. Ladies, you want to know if the man you will marry thinks he is sovereign over his own life—calling the shots without consulting God—or whether he is submitted to Christ.

Listen to me carefully, women. If he is not submitted to Christ, you don't want him. It is easier (I don't want to lie and say it's easy) to submit to a man who is submitted to God. Is he sovereign over his own destiny, or is he submitted to the King of kings and the Lord of lords? Notice I'm asking, "Is he a servant of Christ?" and not, "Does he come to church?" I don't care if he comes to church. I asked if he's *working for Christ,* not whether he is a Christian. I don't care if he's a Christian. There are a lot of Christians who are not surrendered to Christ.

Here is what I am asking: Is there evidence in his life that he can hear and obey God? Is there evidence in his life that God has permission to correct him and redirect his plans? By the way, the only acceptable evidence is that you have seen, and he has shared, aspects of his life that God has corrected.

Is He a Captain or a Crew Hand?

The captain of a ship charts the course. The crew hand is the one who sits around and waits to be told what to do. When the ship hits a storm, the captain is at the helm keeping everyone calm and directing them to safety.

Paul was a captain-type man. Look what happened when the ship he was on faced a storm. The author of Acts explained, "In an attempt to escape from the ship, the sailors let the lifeboat down into the sea, pretending they were going to lower some anchors from the bow. Then Paul said to the centurion and the soldiers, 'Unless these men stay with the ship, you cannot be saved'" (27:30–31).

Women, the man you marry is going to chart the course for your family. Is there evidence that he can make wise decisions? Storms are going to hit your ship. Whether they be miscarriages, layoffs, or sicknesses. You need a captain to guide you through, not a crew hand who may check out emotionally.

Does he have a plan? Do you like his plan? What is he building? Is that what you want to build? If he can't lead his own life, how is he going to lead you and your children? You are setting yourself up for a life of frustration with hazel eyes. I know what you're thinking: *You don't understand, Pastor, he's so dreamy.* Well, close your eyes and move on.

Is He Broke or Burgeoning?

When you're dating, ask the question, "Is he broke or burgeoning?"

I need you to stay with me because I'm not coaching you to be a gold digger. Hang in here.

First, let me explain what that word *burgeoning* means. *Bur-*

geoning means on the verge of blowing up. I mean, if you just wait about half a second, this is going to be a hot commodity. What you're looking for is an IPO, which is a financial term that means "initial public offering." It refers to companies that are about to go public. And if you get in early, you can ride the stock all the way to the top. So maybe somebody starts their own company, and it's small and growing, and then when it's almost about to blow up, they'll offer it on the New York Stock Exchange. And it's a really big deal because if you buy in on that first day, and it becomes a really strong company, you can ride that thing to the top. I heard some people put like two thousand dollars in Yahoo when it first came out. That two thousand turned into two million.

Your man may be the next Yahoo, Amazon, or Tesla. It doesn't necessarily matter where he is right now. What matters is where he's going. Zechariah 4:10 says, "Who dares despise the day of small things?" It's saying: "Do not despise small beginnings." (However, *do* despise small endings.)

I want you to know this because the right man for you might not have a thick wallet today. There is nothing wrong with a man being broke. The question to ask is: Why is he broke? Is he in the police academy, about to graduate and serve his community with integrity and honor? Is he broke because he's finishing up in pharmacy school or completing his cadet training? Or is he broke because he's putting all his money into his rap career? Does he have rims on his car and not a penny in his retirement account?

Sister, if you're starry-eyed about this joker with the rims, if you're insisting that it's all going to be all right, you're only fooling yourself. You're not going to be all right. You're going to be frustrated for the rest of your life. Do you know people say that the number one cause for divorce is money fights and money problems? And it's not that people are gold diggers. It's just that when there's no money, things are really tense and stressful.

The Bible says a man who does not work, who does not provide for his family, is worse than an unbeliever.[2] Now, I'm not saying there's anything wrong with a woman making more than a man. I was talking to this one guy, and he said, "Pastor, I'm sorry, man. I just can't marry a woman that makes more money than me." I said, "You're a fool." I got no problem with a woman making more money than me. Why? Because it's going into our joint account, and I'm going to spend it like I made it!

You are building something together. Not you build your half, I build my half, and we'll meet in the middle. You're building a life together. There is no shame. There is no problem with that. The woman can make more, but if anything were to happen to her, or her desire to work changes, the man must be able to provide.

Is He Humble or the Hulk?

You remember the Hulk? The Hulk is the huge green monster alter ego of Bruce Banner. Banner is a physicist. He's really kind of quiet and introverted until he's stressed out. Until he's ticked off. And then he blows up into this raging green monster called the Hulk.

Ladies, you want a man who can get control of his emotions, anger, rage, and passions. Proverbs 25:28 says, "Like a city whose walls are broken through is a person who lacks self-control."

If a man can't control his anger, he also cannot control his lust. Because it's not an anger problem; it's a *control* problem. One of the reasons it's so important to wait until marriage for sexual intimacy is because if you don't learn to control your passions before marriage, you will continue to not control them in marriage.

If you're a man reading this and you see some of these problem areas in yourself, take them seriously. Don't get married until you handle them. Join a small group. Get around other men of God.

If you're a woman reading this, I need you to not make excuses for men.

"You understand, Pastor. It's not a big deal. He just pushed me once. I mean, he didn't really mean it. He was having a bad day."

Excuse me, sister. There's only one Savior, and He died on the cross. Stop trying to be someone else's Messiah. If the man you are dating is abusive, he needs help you cannot give him. Get out now, and don't look back.

"He just needs somebody in his corner. He never had somebody who could teach him to be a man. And I'm the only one in his life who knows Jesus. I can't leave him."

Nah.

Dating is not ministry, and marriage is not a mission field.

Know Who You're Dealing With

When you're dating, you're dating for a purpose. That purpose? Marriage. And these are the kinds of questions that are going to help you discern whether the person you're getting to know is marriage material.

Okay ladies, you've got a tool now that can help you assess whether a gentleman is prepared to go the distance. And now I'm going to offer a similar tool to the gentlemen. (By all means, listen in!)

Assess Her as a Traveling Companion

Ask These Four Questions

Note: This chapter is for the guys.

A NUMBER OF YEARS AGO, OUR CHURCH PACKED A FIFTEEN-passenger van with young adults to drive to New York for a Jesus Culture conference. I was driving and, although we weren't dating at the time, Zai just happened to be in the front with me. After four hours of talking together—without a single lag in the conversation—I was pretty sure I was in love.

As you search for your co-pilot, you're looking for that person with whom you want to have those conversations—hour after hour, month after month, year after year. And while it's going to take some work to discern that, there are four questions I believe can help you decide whether or not a woman might be that person in your life.

Questions Men Should Ask

Brother, when you're dating, you're dating for a purpose. That purpose? Marriage. So I want you to ask some strategic questions to determine if the woman you're dating is marriage material.

Is She a Sea Breeze or a Tsunami?

A number of folks in my congregation are from the Caribbean. If you've ever been to the Caribbean—maybe Barbados, the Dominican Republic, or the Bahamas—there are few things as peaceful as standing on the beach, in the morning or in the evening, with that breeze blowing over you. It's just a little salty. It's refreshing.

Now, you ever seen a tsunami? A tsunami is out of control—one wave of destruction after the next.

You're looking for a woman who can manage the affairs of her life with poise and grace. Not barely holding on for dear life, ready to rip everyone's head off because her Pop-Tart caught fire in the toaster. The woman you marry should be peaceful and refreshing to be around, not wave of drama after wave of drama after wave of drama. If she cannot manage her own life, she will just bring that chaos into yours. Paul wrote in 2 Thessalonians, "We hear that there are some who walk among you in a disorderly manner, not working at all, but are busybodies" (3:11, NKJV). What are her goals? What is she doing? What has she stuck to for longer than three weeks?

"Oh, I'm working on a master's."

A few weeks later: "I want to be a superstar."

After a couple more weeks pass: "I think I'm going to move to Chicago."

Those can all be great goals, but has she followed through

on any goal or simply jumped from one to the next without any real commitment?

Some of the greatest attributes a woman can have are peace and stability. The woman you are interested in dating doesn't have to have a clear, unshakable ten-year plan, but you do want to be with someone who is working to develop one. And ask yourself honestly, *Is the woman I am dating going to help me reach my goals? Am I prepared to help her meet her goals? Do our goals even align?* And if your answer to that last question is no, you need to have a conversation ASAP to see if you can get on the same page; if you can't, it's time to politely call the relationship off. If you are with someone whose foundation shifts and shakes and changes every single day, you will not be able to build a family that's secure.

Is She a RAV4 or a Roller Coaster?

If you've ever driven in a Toyota RAV4, you know it's a great experience, though it may be a little bumpy sometimes. However, it is far less terrifying than a roller coaster. On a roller coaster, you can't always tell what the next loop, turn, drop, or rise is going to be. It's unpredictable.

Is the woman you're considering a RAV4 or a roller coaster? Specifically, I'm thinking about her emotions and her words.

And let me be clear: The fact that God made women more emotionally sensitive than men is a blessing, not a curse. (No man needs a hardened gangster with "THUG LIFE" tatted on her forearm.) The emotional sensitivity of women is a *gift* from God. But I need you to notice that there's a difference between emotional sensitivity and emotional instability.

There's a great theologian named Vivian Green who wrote a commentary called *Emotional Rollercoaster.* Okay, I'm joking.

She's an R & B singer, and "Emotional Rollercoaster" is one of her songs. The author of Proverbs wrote, "The wise woman builds her house, but with her own hands the foolish one tears hers down" (14:1). There are women who build up those around them, and there are those who tear down everything they see, usually with their words.

When a woman is emotionally unstable, you don't know who you're going to get each day. Guys, you don't want to be asking yourself, *Who is going to show up today? Is it extreme Sasha? Or sweet Sasha?* You need to know who's going to show up to build with you every single day.

I cannot tell you how many women I have encountered who are constantly pulling down their husbands, pulling down their children, and destroying everything that they want to build with their words. Together, you want to be building, not destroying.

Is She a Daughter or Delilah?

Delilah was a seductress in the Bible who used her appearance and flirtation to get everything she wanted. And the author of Judges reported this about a buff dude named Samson:

> Some time later, he fell in love with a woman in the Valley of Sorek whose name was Delilah. The rulers of the Philistines went to her and said, "See if you can lure him into showing you the secret of his great strength and how we can overpower him so we may tie him up and subdue him. Each one of us will give you eleven hundred shekels of silver." (16:4–5)

Samson falls in love with Delilah, and it does *not go well.* Fellas, Samson lost his eyes, his vision, his destiny. Samson lost his life because he fell for the wrong woman. A lot of times, when it comes to finding the right person, people will say that the most important thing is whether or not she's a Christian. And while that's not bad, it's not enough. You need to ask, "Does she know that she's a daughter of the King?" All her needs are met by the King of kings and Lord of lords. A woman whose identity and security are found in Christ knows that God provides everything she needs, so she is neither needy nor independent. She is dependent on her Father for affirmation, attention, and provision.

Let's talk about Super Bowl commercials. Because if the Baltimore Ravens are out, the only good part will be the commercials. Have you ever seen a Rolls-Royce commercial on TV? Nope, because not everyone can afford a Rolls-Royce, so it makes no sense advertising to those who can't purchase one. Now, you've seen a Honda commercial. You've seen the inside of the trunk, the engine, the back seats, the navigation. I want to suggest that a daughter of the King doesn't advertise to everyone because she knows only a few people can "afford her bride price."

Is She Fierce or Fearful?

Fear is one of the greatest barriers to a woman thriving in a marriage. And you want to keep your eyes open for fear when you're dating. She may be wondering,

> *Will I lose my identity or individuality and just get overshadowed?*
> *Will I get taken advantage of?*
> *Will I miss out on all the dreams I had for myself before I met this guy?*
> *Am I supposed to give up on ever being happy again?*

That is a posture of fear. What all of those wonderings have in common is *I*. Let me talk to the ladies who are reading this chapter for a minute: Selfishness will keep you from ever having the marriage or the relationship that God ordained for you. It cannot be I, I, I, I, I. It must be we and us. God said that in marriage the two become one.

You may think that when you get married, you'll disappear. No, that's fear bullying you. But what I'm saying is you have to give up your right to make yourself happy; you have to give up your right to satisfy yourself. But you're not giving that right to your husband! I hope this sets you free: God did not design your spouse to fulfill you or make you happy. Only God can do that. And you're not giving up your rights to a man. You are giving up your rights to God, saying, "God, I trust You for my fulfillment and satisfaction. God, You will make my dreams come to pass. And I'm not going to hold on to them with a vise grip." Marriage is not designed to make you happy or satisfied. God is the only one who can truly satisfy. As long as you are still seeking to satisfy your destiny, you're not fully trusting God to satisfy.

In one of his letters, John wrote, "There is no fear in love. But perfect love drives out fear, because fear has to do with punishment. The one who fears is not made perfect in love."[1] One of the reasons people in our generation are getting married later and later in life is fear. *What if it doesn't work out? What if I'm miserable? What if that person doesn't satisfy me?* I can tell you right now: That person will not satisfy you because that's not what they were designed to do.

If you're going to get over that fear, you're going to have to start looking at God as your fulfillment. And men, listen to me carefully: If the person you're dating is not fulfilled in Christ, you have found a woman who can never be pleased. Run for your life. God has the best for you when you do it His way. When you trust Him.

Know Who You're Dealing With

You know what the destination is: marriage. When you're dating, you want to arrive at your desired destination with the right person. And these are the kinds of questions that are going to help you discern whether the person you're getting to know is marriage material.

In addition to these big-picture questions, I also want to encourage you to go a little deeper in the kinds of conversations you're having before you ever consider saying "I do."

Notice the Mileage

The Nitty-Gritty of What You Can't Not Know

BEFORE ZAI AND I STARTED DATING, SHE'D PLANNED A BIRTHDAY party for me at Olive Garden with a bunch of friends.

Somehow, at the party, the conversation turned to this question: "What's the worst whoopin' you've ever gotten?" And people were chiming in with stories of how their parents disciplined them physically. Of course, there's always that awkward one: the person with no whoopin' stories because they got sent to the time-out corner.

As people were having fun with this conversation, Zai announced, "I don't believe in corporal punishment."

And I was like, "What's corporal punishment?"

Then Zai, who spent the first five years of her life in Sierra Leone, explained, "I think you call it 'spanking' kids."

That's when I decided to push her buttons.

"I don't believe in corporal punishment either," I agreed.

I saw what I thought was a look of approval on her face.

Then I continued, "I don't believe in spanking kids. I believe in *whoopin'* kids."

I was just being a jerk.

Zai answered, "I just think it's wrong."

I went all in.

"Well," I shot back, "I think you're wrong. The Bible says that if you love your kids, you'll discipline them."

"Well," she answered, "the Holy Spirit hasn't convicted me about that yet."

I could have let it go there with her earnest and humble admission. But there was no world in which I was going to let it go there.

"That just means your convict-er is broken."

I was a real treat.

Although I didn't know it at the time, Zai went home and told God, "I can't marry that man. That's a deal-breaker for me. I can't. I can't deal with that."

Guess what? Zai had grown up not seeing the best examples of discipline. She hadn't seen someone who knew how to control their anger. She'd never seen physical discipline done in love. So, eventually, when we were dating seriously, that was something we had to work through. But by the time we got engaged, we were on the same page. (And the first time our son, Roman, threw spaghetti across the room? She was fully on board the discipline train.) That was an important conversation we needed to work through before we got married.

What do you need to see in the person you're with before you can marry them? What are the questions you need to ask of someone before marriage? What is it that you can't *not* know if you're considering committing yourself to someone for a lifetime?

Verify

When you buy a used car, you don't know what you're getting. (No, I'm not calling the person you might marry a used car.) One of the worst car decisions I ever made was buying a beautiful BMW 5 Series with the sport package and 135,000 miles on it. As beautiful as it was, that car started giving me trouble about the minute I drove it off the lot. I'm not going to say it was God's grace when I totaled it thirty days later and the gap insurance kicked in to pay off the loan, but if you said it, I wouldn't argue with you. If there were questions I could have asked before buying that car that might have helped me know it was a bad purchase, I would have asked them.

When it comes to dating and marriage, there actually *are* questions that can give you the intel you need. Before I get to what you need to ask your partner, I want to encourage you to seek verification when they share their answers. Ask the person these questions, but don't take their word for it. Look for proof. People will tell you what you want to hear to get you to do what they want you to do. (And they might not even realize they're doing it!)

When it comes to the kinds of characteristics and qualities that put someone in an unfavorable light, people are only 75 percent honest (at best) when they're dating. Probably more like 50 percent.

Whatever level of anger they show you? It's 75 percent.

Whatever level of selfishness they show you? It's 75 percent.

Whatever level of pride they show you? It's 75 percent.

When you're dating, the other person knows you have the opportunity to leave them, so they're managing perception. Everybody does it.

Everybody.

So if you're dating the person you're going to marry, you're only seeing part of the person who will become your spouse. Ninety days after y'all walk down that aisle though? It is likely going to be a lot closer to 100 percent.

Who in the world are you, and what have you done with that lovely person I was dating?

Maybe it's ninety days. Maybe it's two years. People can hide who they are for two years. Maybe it takes a difficult season in marriage like a job loss or miscarriage. They will eventually show you 100 percent of who they really are.

Even you, Pastor?

I play the piano. When Zai and I were dating, she wanted to learn how to play the piano. So, I gave her piano lessons when we were dating. But once we got married? The lessons stopped.

When Zai and I were dating, I wrote her poems. And over the ten years we've been married? She's gotten . . . one. Okay, don't judge me. I'm going to run and write a poem as soon as I'm done writing this chapter. Zai did it to me as well! For the entire time we were dating, Zai was a pescatarian. Every time we would go out to eat, she would order water, a salad, and maybe dessert. I was able to take her to the most expensive restaurants as soon as I caught on because I knew the bill would never be that high. It couldn't have been six weeks after we got married that she said she missed meat—and, boy, did she make up for lost time!

The point is that most of us are on our best behavior when we're dating.

Know About Their Faith Convictions

Before you get married, I'm assuming that you already know about the faith convictions of your partner. Of course. "Do you believe that the Bible is the infallible Word of God, or do you believe that it's optional? Do you believe it's open for interpretation? Do you think it's culturally irrelevant today?"

That's a great conversation to have, but I'll admit that was pretty specific. Bigger picture, it's better to ask yourself whether this person is submitted to God. Have they ever been challenged about their character during their quiet time with God? And did they do something about it? Has their relationship with God moved them to take steps to be more kind to people or more patient? Have they ever said, "I feel like God is leading me to apologize to my father for the way I spoke to him earlier"? Ask yourself if this person seeks to hear from God and make changes in their life based on God's guidance.

When it comes to hearing from God here, I'm not talking about the differences between someone who grew up in a charismatic Pentecostal church and the Presbyterian they plan to marry. . . . That's not a deal-breaker. But you do need to see that the other person can submit to God. This is a big one.

I'll also suggest that you both agree on what church you're going to go to. Some people think that one's not a big deal, but then after marriage it can become a massively big deal for some couples.

"She's in a church where I am dying spiritually. I can't do it."

"My husband is a deacon at a church that does nothing for me. I don't want to be here. Our kids don't want to be here."

Agree on where you will attend church before you get married. If you can't agree, I think this is a deal-breaker.

Know About Their Sexual History

There are some conversations you need to have before you get married that may feel pretty tender. These are not first-date questions. They're not third-date questions either. These are the intimate conversations you need to have with someone before you join lives. Make sure you have this conversation during your premarital counseling, even if you've had it prior. Some couples believe because they both had an impure sexual history that it won't be a big deal to either of them. "We both repented and are walking in holiness now. What does it matter?" It matters. There is a difference between two sexual partners and nine. You will face challenges when one person has waited for marriage and the other hasn't. You will face challenges even if both of you waited until marriage but pornography played a role in your story (which impacts an alarming number of marriages today). You will face challenges if you both waited but because you came from an ultraconservative background, you only heard sex referred to as "doing the nasty" or described as "dirty" or "ungodly."

Bottom line: Regardless of your story, you will face challenges, so talk about them in a safe place. Challenges like struggling to truly open up and drop your guard sexually around your spouse. Challenges like not desiring to pursue your spouse sexually because intimacy has lost its appeal for you. You will regret it if you do not talk through these types of challenges before marriage.

While it is important to know your partner's *consensual* sexual history, you don't always need the *exact* body count. If the other person didn't wait for marriage, it can be helpful to know whether it was in the neighborhood of one person, or three, twelve, or twenty-five people. You may want to know ranges.

You also need to know if you *know* any of them personally. You don't want to be surprised by that one, and you don't want your spouse to ever be in a situation where they're caught off guard either.

Have You Suffered Physical or Sexual Abuse?

Too many couples find out only after they're married that their partner has suffered physical or sexual abuse, or even suffered the trauma of an abortion. And that's problematic. Just because something happened in the past doesn't mean that it isn't affecting that person today. Well, actually, if you've kept your dating relationship pure, it might *not* be affecting them very much while you're dating. But once you are physically intimate, it's natural for those old hurting places to flare up.

I'm certainly not suggesting that what someone endured in their past needs to be a deal-breaker in any way. But when you know what someone has suffered, you know what you're both getting into. And you know that you need to find resources to help you both navigate these challenges.

Know Other Important Parts of Their Experience That Impact Marriage

No one is coming into marriage with a fresh slate. We all bring experiences, trauma, and expectations into marriage. The more work you can do ahead of time to acknowledge what you are bringing in, the better prepared you will be to create an even healthier dynamic with the person God has for you. Here are some examples of past experiences you would benefit from examining on your journey toward marriage.

What Has Your Experience of Finances Been?

We've all had unique experiences of financial provision and lack, both in our childhood homes and also in adulthood. Every person's experience is unique, and you want to know about your partner's experience before you join in marriage. Once you're married, combined finances are the best way for peace and wealth building, but you must know what you are getting yourself into.

- What were your parents' financial lives like, and how did that impact you?
- What is your current financial situation? How much debt do you have? What's your income?
- What are your *values* when it comes to finances?
- What is your earning potential?
- What are your financial goals?
- When we're married, do you plan on combining incomes?
- What should my expectations be of you working? What are your expectations of me? (These questions are especially relevant if you anticipate having children.)

What Has Your Experience of Marriage Been?

Just as we've all had differing experiences of finances, we've also had wildly different experiences of marriage, even if only in the homes in which we were raised. Get curious about what this person's experience of marriage has been.

- What was your parents' marriage like?
- What marriage did you see that you respected and admired?

- What makes for a good marriage?
- How do we build a good marriage? How do we sustain it?
- Have you been married before? Why did it end?
- Are you still married in another state with a family I don't know about?

How Do You Imagine We'll Grow, or Not Grow, Our Family?

All of us are also likely bringing different expectations of how many children we might want in the future, and it's important to get those expectations out on the table. For example, someone who grew up as an only child and felt lonely at home may want to have four or five children. But someone who grew up with a dozen siblings and felt neglected may want to have just one or two children.

- How many children would you like?
- How affectionate were your parents with you, physically and emotionally?
- Would you be open to fostering or adoption?
- How were you disciplined as a child? How do you intend to discipline our children?
- Are you bringing previous children into the relationship? Will you trust me to parent your children that aren't mine?

While you don't need to talk about how you will raise your future offspring during the first few months of dating, eventually you will want to give some careful thought to your expectations around children and how you will raise them.

Be on the Same Page

Three years into marriage is not the moment to find out your spouse never intended to have children. Any major topics that would directly impact your shared life together need to be discussed before the wedding. Some of these will naturally come up in dating. If they don't, be intentional during your engagement to make sure you've communicated well about them. This would be a great time to tap into your community and ask your Christian friends and mentors what they wish they knew about their spouse before getting married. This could be a sensitive question, so maybe pose it as, "From your experience, what things should I be asking that I may not think to ask?"

There Really Should Be an Instruction Manual . . .

You know how men are usually friends with other men? Of course you do. And you know how women are usually friends with other women? Sure. These kinds of same-sex friendships are one of God's very very *good gifts* to us.

But what about platonic friendships between women and men? Sometimes, for a season, these friendships can be natural and normal, especially in the context of a larger friend group. But we all know that it can get weird, right? It doesn't have to, but it *can*. That's why I want you to be very intentional about how you're navigating these friendships. We've been dishing specifically about the relationships that will lead to marriage, but I also want you to be very purposeful and intentional about those that may not.

Let's do this.

Don't Believe Everything You Hear

You don't need a man.

You're fine single.

Emotional intimacy is not cheating.

Relationships shouldn't be hard work.

You shouldn't have to compromise or sacrifice if you're really with the right person.

Before I say yes to a date, I need to know if he's the one.

If he doesn't give you his passwords, he's cheating.

Read the Instruction Manual

Can Guys and Girls Just Be Friends?

CHARLENE, IN HER EARLY THIRTIES, WAS ONE OF THE WOMEN IN Tyree's friend group of about a dozen young adults. And the two of them were friends. There was never any of that weird "Will they? Won't they?" because Tyree was dating a woman named Courtney when he met Charlene. Sometimes, Tyree would seek "wise counsel" from Charlene. They joked that she was kind of like an informant, helping him understand how women think.

"What is my girlfriend thinking about this?"
"What does she mean when she says this?"
"What should I get her?"

Charlene was happy to play along and let Tyree know her thoughts.

"Well, I think she's really saying this."
"I think I'd want this."

After about ten months, Courtney ended her relationship with Tyree. Eight weeks later, Charlene professed her feelings to Tyree, saying, "I'm really interested in you, and I think we would make an awesome couple. What do you think?"

Tyree wasn't just surprised; he was gobsmacked. He didn't see it coming because he didn't have feelings for Charlene like that.

Ouch.

But when he paused and reviewed their friendship, he saw it. His cousin was in the same friend group, and she'd seen it coming. He confided in her, "I should have known she was interested in me."

In the "Can guys and girls just be friends?" debate, this story falls under "No."

You know how no one ever reads the owner's manual that comes with their car? (If you've never seen it, it's in the glove compartment.) Well, I should say that they don't read it until something goes wrong. Or there's something they can't operate. Both Charlene and Tyree thought their friendship seemed to be going great. Until it wasn't. If they'd read the manual—and by "manual" I do mean this chapter of this book—each of them could have predicted what was coming.

Another Perspective

I do think the question of whether guys and girls can be friends is a little more complicated than a car instruction manual. But in the big picture? I think men and women can and should be friends, especially when they're single. One of the reasons some Christians are single a lot longer than they want to be is because they isolate themselves from the opposite sex in a misguided approach to holiness. I think it's healthy to have friend groups made up of both women and men. *The key to men and women having good friendships is healthy boundaries.*

Having healthy boundaries means that you don't need to be each other's confidants.

You don't need to be texting first thing in the morning or late at night.

You don't need to talk on the phone for hours on end.

Unless you're calling to ask, "Didn't you say you were going to give me a ride home from choir practice?" you don't need to be talking past eight or nine o'clock.

Women and men can be friends when they exercise healthy boundaries that guard their own hearts and guard the hearts of their opposite-sex friends. Our greatest treasure is our time, and our hearts will fall for almost anybody we invest time into, even if it's the wrong person.

And if you're dating someone, you need to be even more stringent with those friend boundaries. You don't need to cut off those friendships, but the person you're dating should feel 100 percent comfortable that those are safe friendships—ones that don't threaten the dating relationship.

So, the answer to the "Can men and women be just friends?" question is a nuanced one.

"Just" Friends?

If you're into old-school rom-coms, the 1989 movie *When Harry Met Sally* poses the question of "Can guys and girls just be friends?" Actually, lots of rom-coms explore this question.

But let's say we're not in rom-com land. Let's say we're in church. There's a myth that guys can't have female friends and women can't have guy friends. You're either dating each other or avoiding each other. *You know I'm right.*

When it comes to having friends of the opposite gender, it's important to keep those healthy boundaries in place. I think we can be friends, but we have to respect those boundaries. For example, if you're both single, you don't need to talk on the phone at eleven o'clock every single night.

If you are on the phone at eleven every night, *pay attention*. Call it what it is. It's likely a little bit more than friendship. And I'm not throwing shade, because we've all seen those kinds of friendships that eventually turn into marriages. That happens, and it's great; just call a spade a spade.

But what you don't want to happen is what happened between Charlene and Tyree—the situation where one person catches feels and the other really is not interested. You might be enjoying the late-night chats, but if you're not feeling it, you are *leading the other person on.*

I remember being a single guy with friends who were girls; I knew that some of them liked me, and I knew that I wasn't feeling it. But the friendship *felt good.* (It does, doesn't it?) It feels good to receive that attention. But if you know that other person is feeling it and you aren't, you need to take a step back.

You don't have to be a mind reader to figure out when someone likes you.

Maybe he comes right out and says it.

Maybe you see it in his eyes.

Maybe her friend tells you she digs you.

Maybe she's speaking in a playful singsong pitch that's an octave higher than her normal voice.

If you and your opposite-sex BFF are spending a lot of time together, if you're communicating daily, you need to pay attention to that. Maybe it means that one of you needs to take a step back. Or maybe it means that one of you needs to take a step forward.

Boundaries

When it comes to having healthy boundaries in opposite-sex friendships, there's what I call the basic rule (though it may not be basic for everyone): If you have a friend of the opposite sex, you do not need to be alone together in a private place. Not in a dorm room. Not in an apartment. Not in an Airbnb.

But there's more.

I'm about to get bold.

I wouldn't say this is a black-and-white rule, but it's a strong slate gray. Nah . . . it's *charcoal*. You ready? Even in public, you shouldn't be going out one-on-one. Here's why: When a man and a woman go out to a nice restaurant as friends? One of them is lying. Again, I don't think anyone is maliciously trying to hurt the other person; I just think that kind of attention feels good, and so we don't want to set up the boundary that would protect our friend from being hurt.

I say it's not a hard-and-fast rule because there are exceptions. For example, let's say you had a friend from Bible study during college. After graduation, she moved to Texas, and you moved to New York. If she has a business trip to New York, you might want to grab food and catch up. Sure. That's not *off-limits*.

Even then, the host and waiter at the restaurant will treat you like a couple. There will probably be the awkward moment when the waiter hands the man the check, assuming he's a gentleman and will pay for the date. Going out one-on-one isn't off-limits, but it's definitely a one-in-a-million type of thing.

But going out frequently when you live in the same city? You're asking for trouble. Even with the best of intentions. I'm going to guess that, even if nobody is saying it, somebody is attracted to someone, and that person is eventually going to feel like they're being led on. They're going to feel like they are being used as an emotional security blanket.

I get that when you're enjoying spending time with a friend of the opposite sex, you might try to justify why it's *right*.

"We're not doing anything *wrong*."

"It's no different than my same-sex friendships."

"It's not like we're having *sex*."

(You may have seven thousand other justifications.)

But if you know it's not going anywhere—whether you're the one who has the feels or not—you really need to step back. It's not about what you're doing, or not doing, with your bodies. The issue is your heart. The issue is *their* heart. Proverbs 4:23 warns, "Above all else, guard your heart, for everything you do flows from it." And when you're developing affection for someone who's not part of your future, you're putting your life on pause for that person. "Yeah, but we didn't have sex." You're giving them your time. "Yeah, but we didn't have sex." You're sharing your emotions. "Yeah, but we didn't have sex." You're offering them your greatest ideas.

You feel me?

Buckle up because it's about to get worse.

Let's say the person you believe is your "soulmate" had their eye on you. They were spying out the land. They were observing how you behave. And when they noticed the closeness you had with this person you have no intention of marrying or dating? It made them believe you had a thing with your friend, and it turned them off! When that happens, you're actually chasing away what you've been asking God for by entertaining what you already know is not the answer to your prayer.

My advice: If you have a close friendship like this with someone of the opposite sex, handle your business. If you're the one who's not feeling it, you don't have to initiate a whole "we need to talk" conversation to tell your friend that you're not interested in them *like that*. Just begin choosing to prioritize other things. Other people. Do it gently.

Is This a Thing?

Maybe you *are* feeling this friendship.

Let's say that you have been talking to someone for a few months. You're getting to know each other. You know if they like dogs or cats. You know if they prefer the Marvel universe or DC Comics. You are learning who they are and what they are about. It's going well. And one or both of you are wondering where it's headed.

Some people may try to say, "I don't want to put a label on it."

Well, guess what? In the Garden of Eden, Adam's first job was to *label* everything he saw.

"This is cow."

"This is dog."

"This is boyfriend."

"This is girlfriend."

You need a label. You need to make it plain. And you know how to make it plain?

"Will you be my girlfriend?"

It's that simple.

For the Guys

Men, if you've been talking for twelve weeks, make it plain. Ask her out, or take a step back. You have to name what it is. The only reason you would not name it is if you know she's not the one but you plan on playing with her heart. Or God has made it clear that she's not the one but you are in rebellion.

For the Ladies

Ladies, if he doesn't ask you out, it's okay for you to ask, "What is this?"

You don't need to say, "I want you to be my boyfriend." What you're saying is, "I've given you enough of my heart that you should know by now what you want to do with it."

It's okay for you to say, "Poop or get off the pot."

Maybe It *Is* a Thing

Although Disney movies have convinced some of us that the fairy tale happens when an unknown prince rides up on a white horse to claim his woman, your story might be different. The story of how you get to the altar *might* begin with a genuine friendship. But, sister, brother, I want to caution you to be very careful with these friendships.

Don't ever intentionally lead the other person on.

Don't feel like you can't speak up if you are being *led on*.

Don't jeopardize a possibility with someone else, who's spying out the land, because you're playing around with someone you know you won't marry.

Be smart. Be kind. Be intentional.

Differences Are Real

This "just friends" advice goes for both women and men. There can be situations where a girl is sending all kinds of signals to a guy friend and other scenarios where a guy might be doing the same thing to a female friend. We can both go off the rails in similar ways. And both women and men need to be smart about how they navigate these friendships.

But I do want to name that there are also specific *differences* in the ways that men and women have been designed by God. Those differences are usually expressed most fully within the covenant of marriage, but I want you to begin noticing and appreciating them now. Not only am I convinced that God has wired men and women a bit differently, but I believe that those differences are very *good*.

I'm curious if you'll agree.

Popular Rom-Coms and the Messages They Might Be Communicating

1. *Hitch*
Takeaway: When you know how women think, you can offer what women want.

2. *What Men Want*
Takeaway: When you know how men think, you can offer what men want.

3. *When Harry Met Sally*
Takeaway: Men and women can't be just friends.

4. *Love and Basketball*
Takeaway: What is meant to be will be.

22

Examine the Wiring

Women and Men *Are* Different

HERE ARE A FEW FUN FACTS.[1]

Men typically have thicker skin than women. (I don't mean they don't let problems get them down. I mean we literally have thicker skin.)

The daily calorie requirement is higher for men than for women.

Men are more prone to being night owls.

Women have larger memory centers in the brain.

And . . . for when it comes time to put a ring on it . . . while the second-longest finger on a man will usually be his ring finger, typically the second-longest finger on a woman is her index finger.

Now you know.

Do I think that men and women have been created, by God, to be different from one another? I do.

But let me start with *not* getting in trouble . . .

Made in the Image of God

Genesis 1:26–27 explains, "God said, 'Let us make mankind in our image.' . . . In the image of God he created them; male and female he created them." What that tells me is that when God finished creating Adam, who was male, God had not yet created the complete image, or representation, of Himself here on earth. And the flip is also true: Eve, *female,* is not the complete image of God here on earth. *Both* were made in God's image. That is God's good design.

When we watch rom-coms, there's this corny sentiment when the main characters get booed up: "You *complete* me." I want to push back on that because we are complete in Christ; you don't need another human being to complete you. That said, the family unit is not going to be fully what God created it to be if it's void of a female or void of a male. There are different things that each brings to the family unit. And we desperately need each other.

As Christians, we'll point to passages like Romans 13 to claim that there's no human authority—such as government—except what God has established. Or we'll get real excited that, in the first century, God *established* the church. But do you know what the first institution God established was? It was the family! And the family is what prepares people for their God-given purpose. God never designed the government to prepare people for their destiny. God didn't even design the church to launch people into destiny. That's also not the purpose of education. God designed the family to *prepare* people for their destiny. My father never forced me or even put pressure on me to follow in his footsteps and work in full-time ministry. Because of that I am careful to follow that same example with my children. I do, however, celebrate the gifts and passions I see God cultivating in my three children. Zai is constantly sharing with our kids how God empowers, leads, and guides His children to live big lives. We are intentional to make our home a launching pad of destiny for our family.

Man's Role

I know this is controversial today, but I believe that God has designed women and men differently. And I think that's a good thing. The reason you wouldn't drive a pickup truck on a racetrack, or a sports car in a snowstorm, is because different types of vehicles are made to perform to their maximum potential in different environments. And I think that the same is true of women and men. Because we're designed differently, we're going to thrive and flourish in different ways.

I believe God designed man for the responsibility of providing for the family. God designed him to be a protector.[2] God designed man to function as a priest, as Jesus did, introducing his family to God.[3] Then he becomes the standard-bearer by establishing the family's values and identity. He's the visionary for the family.[4] That doesn't mean a woman cannot or should not do these things, but the man should carry the weight of responsibility for the family.

Now, he has to lead with love. A vision without affection breeds resentment and rebellion. Nobody cares what you know unless they know that you care. There has to be care and kindness, or else those being led will rebel!

A family that lacks an emotionally healthy man's presence

is, in some ways, deficient. That family is lacking the provision and vision he was created to bring. And here I'm talking about our natural giftings. Of course the Holy Spirit can give us the ability to step outside our natural strengths or weaknesses, but I believe every family needs an emotionally healthy man.

Woman's Role

The woman in the family is, naturally, to be a nurturer. God has wired women to pay attention to the physical and emotional needs of those around them and equipped them to meet many of those needs.[5]

But I want to get spiritual here. I think the woman is, in many ways, the prophetic voice in the household. Think about Mary, the mother of Jesus. She heard what was being said about Jesus, and she held it in her heart. I think that women see what appears impossible as being *possible*. Where men are more intent on putting their hands to the plow, working for what they can achieve and solving problems, they may struggle to believe that what seems impossible can become possible. We struggle more to dream of what can't be seen. But I see the woman as the one who breathes dreams and possibilities and potential into a family. Once again, that doesn't mean that a man cannot or should not do this also, but the woman should carry the weight of this responsibility for the family.

A family that lacks a woman's presence is, in some ways, deficient. I'm thinking of the sensitivity a woman brings to a family. Now, men can learn to be sensitive, but it's often not our natural strength. A family needs feminine presence. Think of the von Trapp family in *The Sound of Music*. If you are not familiar with the movie, it tells the story of a retired naval officer who is a widower raising seven children using strict military discipline. Sister Maria, a young woman studying to become a nun, is hired to help care for the children; she brings much-needed warmth and joy to the home. And here, again, I'm referring to our natural giftings. But, of course, the Holy Spirit can give us the ability to step outside our natural strengths or weaknesses.

Every family needs a woman.

The Rub

The moment anyone mentions submission of wives to husbands, a lot of people—often women!—feel some kind of way about it. I get it.

But the order we see in Scripture never diminishes women. In fact, the Bible actually offers this beautiful snapshot of an esteemed woman who is a *boss*. You can find it in Proverbs 31. This bad boss is managing her home, overseeing employees, introducing new products to the market, and creating an environment of peace so that her husband can have a political position and command respect in the community. I know this, for certain, because I'm married to one of these Proverbs 31 boss women.

Don't assume that the Bible has only antiquated things to say about human relationships. Assume it has *true* things to say about human relationships.

It is actually very easy to submit to a man who is submitted to God. It is a pain in the neck to submit to a man who is not submitted to God. The dating season is your time to figure out if this guy is submitted to God, because once you say "I do," you have to submit whether he is submitted to God or not. If he is surrendered to his Creator, God will make sure that he's a blessing to your life and not a curse.

While Paul previously encouraged husbands and wives to mutually submit to one another in Ephesians 5:21, the primary command he gives to men in this chapter is not to submit but to lay down their lives.

Basically, we have to die!

Okay, not literally, but Ephesians 5:25 says, "Husbands, this means love your wives, just as Christ loved the church. He gave up his life for her" (NLT). Our responsibility is to make our personal hopes, dreams, and ambitions secondary to serving our wife and championing all that God has made her to be. This can be terrifying. Especially if we are not certain our dreams will ever come to pass or if our wife will take advantage of our serving position. But just as for the woman, when you pick a spouse who is submitted to God, it is dramatically easier.

As we wrap up our journey together, I want you to keep the destination in sight: a marriage where a husband blesses a wife, and a wife blesses a husband, and a couple blesses their family and the world God loves. I am here to testify that it is a truly beautiful ride. So I want to close by giving you a final glimpse at the destination that is worth every mile of the journey.

Pickup Lines

"Girl, you must be tired because you've been running through my mind all day." (This one is a classic.)

"If you were a vegetable, you'd be a *cute*cumber."

"Is your name Faith? Cause you're the substance of things I've hoped for."

"Do you like raisins? How do you feel about a date?"

"I'm usually not very prophetic, but I can see us together."

23

Arrive Safely

You Got This

WHEN I WAS A KID, MY FAMILY WOULD DRIVE ABOUT FOUR HOURS north to visit my grandmother in New Jersey for Christmas. "Four hours" was if we didn't take any breaks. And if there wasn't traffic. And if there weren't any accidents being cleared off the road. You can imagine that with five kids squeezed in the car—who needed to take bathroom breaks and eat and get on one another's last nerves—the trip could be pretty grueling. And we couldn't leave until my dad got off work at five or six. But when we finally pulled into Grandma's driveway and saw her waiting on the porch, we knew we'd made it to paradise. No matter what time we arrived, dinner was waiting. There was hot stew chicken, peas and rice, fried flying fish, and fresh-baked ham waiting to be eaten. It was everything you would expect at midnight in a proper Caribbean home.

The destination made the journey worth every moment.

Remember Zai and I singing and shouting and dancing on the kitchen counters? Moments like those are what make this whole dating journey *worth every bad date along the way.* It's what makes purity worth the wait. The destination—a strong, healthy marriage—is what makes every mile you're traveling worth it. Pastor Jimmy Evans describes marriage as "the safest and most beautiful relationship in the world . . . when you do it God's way."[1] So keep your eyes on the prize.

The destination you're headed toward is a good one. And as you're on this journey, I want to encourage you to never stop trusting God. Remember what Ephesians 3:20 says: "Now to Him who is able to do exceedingly abundantly above all that we ask or think, according to the power that works in us . . ." (NKJV). Regardless of what you can or cannot see, regardless of whether things have gone your way or not, God is in control, and He promised the result is going to be above anything you asked or thought.

While you wait for God's "exceedingly abundantly above," make sure to live life to the fullest. Grow. Laugh. Cry. Risk. Fail. Bounce back. Risk again. Succeed. Celebrate. Don't wait on marriage to start enjoying and living this amazing life God has given you. When that right person does turn up, and marriage comes knocking at your door, let them find you not seated, awaiting their arrival, but up running toward your next adventure.

Don't forget to guard your heart. Proverbs 4:23 says, "Above all else, guard your heart, for everything you do flows from it." Don't just guard against heartbreak or toxic relationships; be mindful to guard against apathy, cynicism, and any thought or emotion that doesn't have you expecting the best.

Finally, love people well. The people you date and the people you don't. The friends you have and strangers you happen to encounter. Just remember that what you do for another person, even if it does not move you any closer to your intended outcome, is truly an act of service to God. Matthew 25:40 says, "The King will say, 'I tell you the truth, when you did it to one of the least of these my brothers and sisters, you were doing it to me!'"(NLT). Every day you have an opportunity to serve God by serving the person He sends across your path. God will always respond and reward you for how you bless others. Mile by mile and turn by turn, make good choices that honor God, honor yourself, and honor others. You can do this.

If you follow the road map, you will get there safely.

Notes

Introduction: Are You Ready for This Journey?

1. See Ephesians 5:22–33.
2. Proverbs 31:10, MSG.
3. Psalm 84:11, KJV.

Chapter 1: Begin with Your Destination in Mind: Know Where You Want to End Up

1. Genesis 2:18.
2. See Proverbs 17:22.

Chapter 2: Check Your Engine: Don't Start the Journey Deficient

1. Les Parrott and Leslie Parrott, *Healthy Me, Healthy Us: Your Relationships Are Only as Strong as You Are* (Nashville: Thomas Nelson, 2020), 159.
2. Psalm 68:6, NLT.
3. 2 Timothy 1:7, NKJV.
4. Matthew 6:21.
5. John 16:33.

Chapter 4: Hit the Road, Women: Be Brave and Put Yourself Out There

1. Proverbs 18:22, CSB.
2. 2 Kings 4:1–7.

3. "Look Inside Victoria Osteen's Life, New Book," KVUE, October 20, 2009, www.kvue.com/article/news/local/look -inside-victoria-osteens-life-new-book/269-345607108.

Chapter 6: Avoid These Obstacles: Steer Around Roadkill and Other Roadside Hazards

1. Brittany Renner (@thebrittanyrenner), "I'm patient because I'm worth the wait," TikTok, December 4, 2022, www.tiktok .com/@thebrittanyrenner/video/7173465812949404971.
2. Evie B., "Brittany Renner Regrets Sleeping with Men Who Didn't Value Her, Blames Failed Relationships on Lack of Self-Worth: 'I've Never Valued Myself,'" Yahoo News, December 22, 2022, www.yahoo.com/news/brittany-renner-regrets -sleeping-men-004331494.html.
3. See Matthew 6:21.

Chapter 7: Trust the Guardrails: What to Look for in a Mate

1. See Genesis 2:18.

Chapter 9: Watch Your Speed: Date at the Right Pace

1. Ephesians 5:22.

Chapter 10: Heed the Warning Signs: Don't Ignore the Cautionary Flags

1. 1 John 1:5–7.
2. "Gen-Z Dating Terms You Probably Don't Know About!," The Wellness Corner, accessed August 15, 2024, www .thewellnesscorner.com/blog/gen-z-dating-terms.

Chapter 11: Travel with Others: Do Not Date in Isolation

1. 1 Samuel 18.
2. Psalm 68:6.
3. This one is a lyric from a Drake song. Drake, featuring T. I. and Swizz Beatz, "Fancy," track 7 on Drake, *Thank Me*

Later, Young Money Entertainment, Cash Money Records, Universal Motown Records, 2010.

Chapter 12: Rely on Seasoned Travelers: Seek the Wisdom of Older Mentors

1. 1 Corinthians 11:1.
2. See Jeremiah 17:9.

Chapter 15: Use Your Signals: The Dating Phase of Dating

1. See Ephesians 5:22.

Chapter 16: Choose a Co-Pilot: The Engagement Phase of Dating

1. Dave Ramsey, "The size of a diamond on an engagement ring does not indicate the future success of a marriage," Facebook, October 12, 2023, www.facebook.com/daveramsey/posts/the-size-of-a-diamond-on-an-engagement-ring-does-not-indicate-the-future-success/882277993261816.
2. Ephesians 5:25.
3. Ephesians 5:22.
4. Jeff Diamant, "Half of U.S. Christians Say Casual Sex Between Consenting Adults Is Sometimes or Always Acceptable," Pew Research Center, August 31, 2020, www.pewresearch.org/short-reads/2020/08/31/half-of-u-s-christians-say-casual-sex-between-consenting-adults-is-sometimes-or-always-acceptable.
5. See 1 Corinthians 13:4.

Chapter 18: Assess Him as a Traveling Companion: Ask These Four Questions

1. See Ephesians 5:21–33.
2. See 1 Timothy 5:8.

Chapter 19: Assess Her as a Traveling Companion: Ask These Four Questions

1. 1 John 4:18.

Chapter 22: Examine the Wiring: Women and Men *Are* Different

1. "25 Fun Facts About What Makes Men and Women Different," Ask the Scientists, https://askthescientists.com/men-women-different.
2. See Ephesians 5:28; 1 Peter 3:7.
3. See Ephesians 5:25–26.
4. See 1 Corinthians 11:1–3.
5. See Titus 2:4.

Chapter 23: Arrive Safely: You Got This

1. Jimmy Evans, "Together Forever: Marriage God's Way; The Most Important Issue in Marriage," Trinity Fellowship Church, YouTube video, April 8, 2024, www.youtube.com/watch?v=nnnKC2GS3TQ.

About the Author

STEPHEN CHANDLER is the senior pastor of Union Church based in Maryland and the author of the bestselling book *Stop Waiting for Permission*. Since 2011, Union has grown from a group of fifty to tens of thousands of people in weekly attendance, with tens of thousands more joining live online every week and was named the fastest-growing church in America by *Outreach* magazine. Stephen is obsessed with people, systems, and culture. A sought-after international speaker, he is unapologetic about helping people maximize their God-given passion. Stephen's true legacy is his family—his three beautiful children, Zoe, Roman, and Jade—with his wife, Zai.

About the Type

This book was set in Bembo, a typeface based on an old-style Roman face that was used for Cardinal Pietro Bembo's tract *De Aetna* in 1495. Bembo was cut by Francesco Griffo (1450–1518) in the early sixteenth century for Italian Renaissance printer and publisher Aldus Manutius (1449–1515). The Lanston Monotype Company of Philadelphia brought the well-proportioned letterforms of Bembo to the United States in the 1930s.

MAXIMIZE YOUR GOD-GIVEN GREATNESS

A powerful road map for scaling the heights of your calling, mapping out the territory of your purpose, and unlocking your greatest purpose in life.

Take a deeper dive into rich lessons with this companion study guide. Discover detailed tips and key tools to help you unlock your inner genius.

 **WATERBROOK**

Learn more about Stephen Chandler's books at
waterbrookmultnomah.com.

Practical, Biblical Guidance for Every Step of Your Relationship Journey

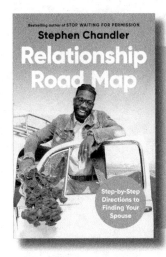

The dating scene can feel disorienting and overwhelming—the apps can make you feel like there are too many options while your experience tells you there are none. Despite these challenges, you can learn how to date thoughtfully and intentionally, all while keeping your character and integrity intact.

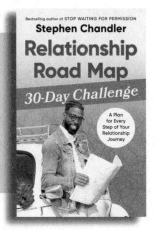

The practical companion guide to *Relationship Road Map*, offering a plan for every step of your relationship journey—from single to dating to engaged to married.